Me
vs
Brain

Me

vs

Brain

AN OVERTHINKER'S
GUIDE TO LIFE

Hayley Morris

CENTURY

12

Century
20 Vauxhall Bridge Road
London SW1V 2SA

Century is part of the Penguin Random House group of companies
whose addresses can be found at global.penguinrandomhouse.com

Penguin
Random House
UK

First published by Century in 2023

www.penguin.co.uk

A CIP catalogue record for this book is available from the British Library.

ISBN 9781529196047

Typeset in 13.5/16 pt Garamond MT Std by Jouve (UK), Milton Keynes
Printed and bound in Great Britain by Clays Ltd, Elcograf S.p.A.

The authorised representative in the EEA is Penguin Random House Ireland,
Morrison Chambers, 32 Nassau Street, Dublin D02 YH68

www.greenpenguin.co.uk

Penguin Random House is committed to a sustainable future
for our business, our readers and our planet. This book is made
from Forest Stewardship Council® certified paper.

For my Dad,
sorry this book mentions queefing and poop
so many times.

Contents

Introduction   xi

Me vs Intrusive Thoughts   1

How Brain Interprets a Text Exchange   11

Me vs Identity   15

Weird Lies I Told about My Rabbit   25

Ten Weird Things that Everyone Does
    (and if You Don't, You Should)   29

Brain vs Puberty   35

Me vs Period   46

Fictional Characters I've Fancied   54

Brain vs Lungs   58

Brain vs The Salon   71

Brain vs Speculum   80

How to Cover Up a Fart   88

Vagina's Lullaby   93

CONTENTS

Brain vs Health Anxiety   101

Definitely True Facts about Brain   114

Brain vs Poop   116

How to Get Over a Break-Up   126

Brain vs Uterus   129

Heart vs Vagina vs Uterus   137

How to Enter a Room like a Normal Person   147

Sex Positions for Anxious People   151

Baby Name Ideas based on My Primary School
    Classmates   154

Brain vs Flying   157

Buying a Coffee   171

How to Defeat Imposter Syndrome   174

Safe Conversation Starters   178

Brain vs Body   181

Brain vs Presentation   184

Brain's Advent Calendar   193

A Fresh Start   198

Things My Brain Thinks about During Sex   202

How to Enjoy Sex as a Grown-Up   206

Me vs Face   209

Me vs Hormones   219

Brain vs Ballistic Missile   226

CONTENTS

Brain vs Gut   234

Dad vs Brain   246

Me vs Grief   254

Brain vs Date   266

Me vs Therapy   275

Me and Brain   281

Acknowledgements   285

Hello, I'm Hayley!

When the good people at Penguin invited me to write this book, the first thing I thought was:

Hell yeah! I'd love to write a book! Sign me up, I'll have a million pages over to you by Wednesday. In fact, make that two million! How big is a book? What do you write about in a book? If I use the same word over and over again will it still look like a word or will I freak out and spiral? Blank pages are quite inspiring, apparently – maybe this'll be the greatest book ever written.

Minutes later, the panic came creeping in. As soon as I put the first words – these words – down on the page, I started to wonder if perhaps I had no idea what I was doing. What if writing a book was really hard? What if I wasn't good enough? As a people-pleaser and Incredibly Anxious Hot Girl™, I spend most of my life thinking thoughts like this. Then I remembered some words of advice that may or may not have been said by very popular writer Ernest Hemingway: 'Write drunk, edit sober.'

Look, if that old, now-dead guy can write loads of books while totally hammered, then surely so can I. Plus, I've got an editor, so I never have to stop drinking. Much like normal life. No, I'm kidding, I'm actually quite boring and cannot stand hangovers.

As I sit here with my silly little hands on my silly little keyboard and tap away, I realise that none of us really knows what we're doing. At least I hope you don't, because otherwise it's just me who's fumbling through life one mistake at a time. Sure, I'm second-guessing every word I type, but maybe that's just how it's supposed to go.

You see, for as long as I can remember, my head has been filled with noise. Not soundtracks to popular movies or words of advice from kindly spirit guides, but one particular voice. For some time I assumed this was my inner child, but then I realised my inner child couldn't possibly be so mean – all the memories I have of myself from childhood suggest I was quite a sweet little thing. This voice mostly tells me that I can't do things. But that's not all. Sometimes I'll be washing the dishes when, out of nowhere, the voice will suddenly say something like: *You're going to die.*

Now, I'm not claiming that I'm never going to die. I am. In fact, we all are (welcome to my book, I promise it won't all be this sinister), but do I need to think about the inescapable reality of death while I'm just giving a dinner plate a little bubble bath? I don't think so. All through the day, this voice will pipe up with observations, reminders and distractions, from the mundane to the bleak:

Your boyfriend doesn't love you.

If the next car you see is blue you will get the job of your dreams, but if it's not you'll be miserable forever.

Everyone you love is going to die.

Those jeans make you look like Rumpelstiltskin and not in a good way.

Sometimes the voice is right – I do occasionally dress like Rumpelstiltskin and not in a good way, but so what? Maybe I want to dress like him; that could become a new trend one day, and I won't have to buy any new clothes for once. Fashion is weird and maybe you're not supposed to play by the rules (probably a direct quote from a Giorgio Armani advert).

When I lay my head on my pillow at night, the voice gets really loud. It keeps me up into the early hours, whispering in my ear about the things I'm most afraid of, while also reminding me how little sleep I'll get if I go to sleep now or in an hour's time, all the way until my alarm goes off. In the morning, when I'm completely exhausted, it tells me I shouldn't have stayed up all night thinking and that we should now call in sick and go to sleep. I can't win.

The voice comes from inside my head, but it isn't me. It's Brain. I, Hayley, am a well-balanced, calm and relatively good person, I think. Brain is not. She's scatty, annoying and wrong about basically everything. I wouldn't say Brain and I are friends – we're more like flatmates in that she lives in my head rent-free and uses all my stuff without asking. She also sleeps in my bed, and that, if you ask me, is a bit too intimate for any flatmate. If I could, I'd get brain surgery to completely remove Brain from my skull. Then she could live in a jar on my desk all pickled and cute and I could be happy for once.

> BRAIN: You can't just put me in a jar on your desk. You'd die, and I know you don't want to die because every time I tell you we're going to die you tell me we're not, we're fine. Which is weird because you literally just admitted that you are going to die eventually.

The thing is, Brain has been there with me through everything – though usually messing things up. She's always putting me down, finding the negatives and causing mischief to make me look like an idiot in public settings. And because of this I have had to change my doctor, dentist and hairdresser – I simply cannot endure the embarrassment of going back to these places. Perhaps you have a Brain like this too, so you know what I'm talking about. If you don't, then this book is going to be truly eye-opening. Welcome to the world of overthinkers.

This book is all about my journey with my very stressful, chatty Brain, as we've learned to navigate life together. My hope is that by reading it, you may recognise some things about your Brain too; it might even help you feel like you're normal. Maybe one day we can all work together as people and Brains to create a better world for everyone.

BRAIN: Eurgh, that was a disgustingly cringeworthy thing to say. Please take my name out of the title, I don't want to be associated with that. In fact, maybe you shouldn't write this book after all.

Too late, I'm already doing it . . .

Me vs Intrusive Thoughts

I have always enjoyed spectating a little drama. My perfect evening's entertainment would look something like this . . .

ACT 1

An argument between a couple at a restaurant when you know the guy has messed up really badly and the girl has him sussed.

ACT 2

An altercation at a local pub when the customer has to be right, but the bar staff aren't paid enough to put up with complaints and do not give in.

ACT 3

A full-on fist fight on the bus between a teen who is loudly playing a game on his phone and a woman who thinks that public transport should be a location for silent meditation.

Drama in my own life, however? No thanks, my friend. That is not for me.

That's not to say I'm not the main character in my own existence. As a teenager, I would walk around my house playing up to the imaginary cameras on my imaginary reality TV show, 'Hanging in the House with Hayley'. I'd talk through my incredibly basic and painfully average make-up routine like a blogger, and cook dinner as though my legions of fans were following along at home. Sometimes, I'd even start to worry that my crush might be watching my imaginary output and load the dishwasher even more seductively than usual. Oops, did I just slut-drop to get that detergent tab? That was for you, Nathan.

I first realised that I'm the main character because of what I initially called The Voiceover. Every day, from morning to night, I would hear a voice that didn't belong to me narrating my every move. I was living inside my own personal movie trailer, but I didn't feel like a star. The first time it happened, I was six years old. I'd been watching a lot of that particularly sad era of Disney films that seemed to hinge mostly on small animals' parents dying. Why did anyone think those were a good idea? Was that supposed to be how parents taught their kids about death? Pretty traumatising if you ask me. I still mourn the loss of Bambi's mum (spoiler alert).

One night, just as I was slipping off to sleep, I suddenly

heard The Voiceover, clear as day, whisper in my ear: *Imagine if your parents died.* Where did it come from? I didn't know. It wasn't my voice, nor my mum nor dad's, and it wasn't the voice of any of the Disney characters I'd seen. I'd never had a thought like that before. Until that moment, my parents dying wasn't something I'd ever considered. I cried myself to sleep, unable to imagine a world without my parents in it.

As I got older, The Voiceover became a constant feature in my life. From the moment I woke up to the moment I fell asleep, I'd hear it, describing my day, asking me questions, and giving me new, often terrifying things to think about.

Around my fifteenth birthday, I got my first ever job as a waitress. Mostly The Voiceover would be quiet at work, as I got on with routine, mundane tasks. It was on a normal Saturday, as I was carrying some glasses to a customer, that I suddenly heard her say, *Imagine if you tripped over now and landed face-first in a pile of smashed up glass?*

For the first time, I felt strongly that she was describing something that was actually about to happen. Some kind of premonition. Voiceovers have a big job in films – they set the scene, they explain everything that happened before the very moment we enter into, and of course they also introduce vital information about the main character. Perhaps even information that I didn't know about myself yet. I rushed to put the tray down and busied myself with a new task: cleaning cutlery.

Immediately, The Voiceover piped up again. *Polishing*

the steak knives, eh? Pretty sharp. Bet that would hurt if you acci-
dentally stabbed yourself in the stomach with one. That day, the
steak knives remained unpolished, the glassware didn't
make it to the table, and I . . . Well, unsurprisingly, I lost
my job.

When I turned seventeen and it was time to learn
to drive, my dad offered to teach me in the car I'd just
bought myself. He'd already taught my brother, who'd
passed – not first time, but he made it on the second
attempt – so I knew I was in safe hands. With my dad
beside me, talking me through each turn and brake, I felt
confident. So confident, in fact, that I passed my test only
three months later. I was finally let loose to drive, wild
and free, around the Isle of Wight.

With the music blaring, I sped along my favourite
roads, with beautiful green fields that looked like they
never ended on one side and the gorgeous blue ocean on
the other. And between me and the ocean? Just a massive
drop and a cliff edge. No. Big. Deal.

Swerve the car off the cliff edge.

What? Oh my God! What? I turn the music down so
I can see better. How close am I to the cliff edge? I need
to stop. I am a danger to myself. I should call someone
and be driven home. I pull over into a dusty car park a
few metres away from where The Voiceover had spoken
and pick up my phone. Should I call my parents? What
would I even tell them?

It's a Catch-22. I am scared that if I start the engine
again I will drive off a cliff, but if I explain to my parents

that The Voiceover told me to drive off a cliff, they would take away my licence and tell me to sell my car. I would lose my freedom and have to resort to public transport which, on the Isle of Wight, was pretty much non-existent.

I put my phone back in the glove compartment, hit the CD player, and mirror-signal-manoeuvre out of the car park. I can't lose my freedom, hell no! I scream-sing 'Unwritten' by Natasha Bedingfield over and over again for the entire journey home. If The Voiceover is still speaking, I just won't listen.

Weeks later, I find myself on the motorway heading to Brighton to start university. It is glorious. The road is three lanes wide, and I know I am made for the fast lane. I live for the thrill of driving over the island-wide 50 mph limit. I am listening to a CD (Voiceover blocker), but when the final track finishes I barely notice. I am fully absorbed in how much I am enjoying the drive and the feeling of freedom.

SLAM ON THE BRAKES.

The Voiceover comes out of nowhere, thick and fast.

*SWERVE INTO THE MIDDLE BARRIER!
FLIP THE CAR!*

PULL UP THE HANDBRAKE.

The wheel wobbles as I tighten my grip. I carefully shift into the slow lane. Over my shoulder, The Voiceover whispers:

Open the door, roll out of the car.

I fumble for the CD player. I need to drown her out. The Voiceover is a menace — she doesn't want me to thrive and be well, she wants thrills, danger and maybe death. Realising this, I ditch the music and focus on the road. I try to ignore her. As I've driven about 10 mph the entire way, I am an hour later than expected, I arrive at my student house and practically kiss the ground. I'm so thankful I've made it.

At uni, The Voiceover becomes my constant companion. I start to feel like I am living in the *Final Destination* franchise – a movie series in which a group of teenagers initially dodge, but then are stalked by, death. It's the last thing you need during Freshers' Week.

Every day, The Voiceover tells me to leap out of windows, dive off balconies and step in front of trains. Every day I resist. She also tells me to do absurd things. To throw my phone out of the window, lick the bird poo on car doors, or spit in someone's drink. One day, I have a one-on-one session with my lecturer and am trying to answer a question about an essay I'd submitted about how the internet is taking over TV. My lecturer has a lot of questions. The voiceover pops into my head again:

Kiss her.

This is new. Where has this come from? Am I in love with my lecturer? Have I developed inappropriate feelings for her? Is this the start of my university's biggest love scandal, all centred around me. Suddenly I am picturing us in wedding dresses, wondering whether she'll lose her job. Will she end up resenting me when she has to choose between the love of her life or the love of her career. This will not end well.

My lecturer carries on talking to me about the project:

'You see here I think it's really interesting that you compare the—'

The Voiceover interrupts again. *Go on, just kiss her on the lips.*

No, stop it! I'm not doing that.

Then slap her on the forehead.

Are you joking? Obviously I'm not going to slap her on the forehead. Can you imagine what she'd do? I'd be kicked out of uni. I'd *rather* kiss her.

My lecturer has fallen silent.

She can hear what we're thinking.

What? She can't can she?

My lecturer is looking at me blankly. 'So what do you think?'

The Voiceover tells me to shout 'cunt' and leave the room, which in this moment seems like my only option. I tell the lecturer I have a headache and I wasn't paying attention. She is visibly annoyed with me – our first lovers' quarrel? She dismisses me from the feedback session and calls in the next student.

I struggle through my degree. I get on with my life. The Voiceover is always with me.

One of my friends has her first baby, and as I'm holding this cute little button-nosed, fresh-out-the-womb angel, I hear, *Drop it.*

I freeze in horror.

Drop kick it.

Without warning, I thrust this delicate little cherub

back into my friend's arms. I cannot be trusted with anything.

I'm not doing what The Voiceover said, but I am listening to her now. More closely than ever. I can't risk not paying attention. Maybe I am the type of person who would kiss their lecturer, drop a baby or drive their car off a cliff. I heed her warnings, every second of every day.

Years later, after a lot of Voiceover torture, I finally decide it's time to tell someone about The Voiceover. As soon as I have the idea, I can't believe I've never thought of it before. I'm almost surprised The Voiceover didn't suggest it herself. After all, what's more self-sabotaging than admitting your deepest, darkest secret? Though maybe she thought if I did tell someone I'd end up being carted away, heavily sedated, and she'd end up being slowly phased out.

As my best friend and I walk along the sea wall I turn to her and tell her everything. It comes out like word vomit, and I watch her face search mine as it all spills out.

There's a long silence. Then she speaks. 'I've imagined pushing you off this sea wall about eight times since we started this walk.'

My God, what a monster, she wants to kill me. Oh wait, no . . . Is she . . .? Are we . . .? I mean, is the reason we're friends because we're both potentially psychopaths?

We turn to Google and discover there is a whole world of people out there who also live with The Voiceover. Only it's not called that, it's called 'intrusive thoughts'. In French it's *l'appel du vide*, which actually sounds kind of sexy and mysterious.

And it turns out that intrusive thoughts are remarkably normal. They don't mean you want to kill yourself, or kill other people. They're just that – thoughts. There are a whole host of intrusive thoughts you can have. It's a fun Russian roulette in terms of what you'll receive. Your intrusive thoughts might be that you're not good enough, worthy enough, sexy enough, funny enough . . . The Voiceover will say stuff like, 'You'll never get that pay rise'; 'You're not a good enough painter to be an artist'; 'You are a worthless piece of shit and everyone hates you.' The normal fun stuff.

You might have intrusive thoughts about sexual things that feel inappropriate and perverted, like, I don't know, kissing your uni lecturer or imagining how couples have sex. This is particularly worrisome when it's about people you'd never normally think about having sex, like the old couple who always sit on the bench by your house. Good for them, of course. I'm glad they've still got spark and mobility. But I'd rather not think about it in great detail. It's quite hard to look two elderly people in the eye after your intrusive thoughts have told you to picture them 69-ing.

I learned that rather than trying to do you harm, these thoughts are your brain's way of protecting you by imagining the worst possible thing that could happen. In fact, it's probably the opposite of what you really want to do. Which makes me feel better about having thought of what Betty and Norman might get up to behind closed doors.

As I start to explore these new ideas, I decide to stand up to The Voiceover, or as I now know her, Brain. She's part of me, but not all of me. Sometimes we think the same, sometimes we don't. Sometimes she's right, but mostly I think she's wrong.

It is now Me vs Brain.

How Brain Interprets a Text Exchange

It's Monday. I've left my boyfriend in bed, crept out of the house and headed to my car, ready for a day at work. I didn't get a chance to say goodbye because I was too absorbed in watching an early-morning argument between two of my neighbours. Now I'm late for work and I'm not 100 per cent sure I put deodorant on. I do the smell test, lightly and very discreetly dragging my finger along my armpit, then subtly bringing it towards my nose for a whiff, all under the guise of scratching my nose. Can confirm I did forget to put on deodorant. Rats!

My phone pings and lights up with a text from my boyfriend.

BOYFRIEND: Morning

BRAIN: Hang on a second, that seems a bit blunt, doesn't it?

I re-read the message three times.

Maybe it was a chirpy: 'Morn-ing!', almost like a sing-song?

BRAIN: If that was the case, he would have put an exclamation mark. He's mad at us, and you know it.

Perhaps it was more like, 'MORNING'. Short, simple, to the point, like when he wakes up and says it to me in person?

BRAIN: Definitely not. Where's the smiley face emoji? He is livid.

Maybe he is angry at me. I type out my reply: Good morning, how are you today?

BOYFRIEND: Good, how are you?

BRAIN: Wow! He's seething with fury. He didn't even say thank you!

I think that seems like a pretty reasonable reply to my question, no?

BRAIN: Nah, definitely not. He's clearly got a problem with us leaving without saying goodbye. He thinks we abandoned him and he thinks we stink.

I panic, and not just because I have forgotten to wear deodorant. Have I upset him? I should apologise just to make sure.

I'm good, thank you. Sorry I left without saying goodbye! Janine and Bill were arguing over the bins again.

BOYFRIEND: Fair, no worries, I've just got up.

BRAIN: Jesus, he's using a full stop? Call the police. This is bad. Very bad.

What do you mean? That's basic punctuation.

BRAIN: Yeah, when you're writing an email. Not when you're texting the love of our life.

You know what, you're being ridiculous. Everything is fine.

BRAIN: If it's so fine, why don't you ask him if he's annoyed at us?

OK, I will . . .

Ah, fair enough! Just wanted to check, is everything OK between us?

BOYFRIEND: Yeah, why wouldn't it be?

BRAIN: Fucking hell, now you've really done it! The break-up text is absolutely on the way. Probe him.

How did things go so south so quickly? A minute ago we were just saying good morning to each other, and now we're breaking up? I quickly type my reply . . .

You just seem a bit off, that's all. Are you sure you're OK?

> BOYFRIEND: I'm fine. Definitely not off.
>
> BRAIN: Bloody. Hell. Double full stops. We're a goner. Tell him we know about the full stops!

I'm riled up. How dare he be so mad at me for not saying goodbye to him this morning? He's got me sweating and I'm fearful of the stench I may now be emitting. I'm late for work! I don't want to get another strike on my record.

I just think it's funny how you're using so many full stops and acting like everything's fine when it clearly isn't.

> BOYFRIEND: Hayley, you're using full stops in your messages to me. I told you everything's OK. Is everything OK with you?
>
> BRAIN: Oh, he wants a fight. Let's give it to him.

My phone rings, it's my boyfriend.
On the phone he tells me everything is fine. He's right, it is fine. He's not mad at me at all!

> BRAIN: Yeah. Unless he's hiding it.

Me vs Identity

I loved being a kid. Being a kid is easy. Your parents wake you up, pick out your clothes, make your food and escort you wherever you need to go. Being a kid is like being a tiny queen with giant servants. You never, ever have to make a single decision.

As an adult, I spend an embarrassing amount of time getting ready to leave the house. It starts easily enough, as I sit in front of my mirror and do my make-up for the day. I always wear my make-up exactly the same. This is partly because I'm rubbish at doing it, but mostly because it's one less decision in the endless decision tree of life. If I learn how to do a smoky eye, cut crease, full glam or barely-there make-up, the branches of the tree won't stop growing. In my case, ignorance is efficiency. Then I style my hair one of two ways: down and wavy, or scraped back into a low bun using the grease from my own head. So far, so good.

The next step is where things get hazy, angry and downright messy. I fling open my wardrobe to reveal an array of clothes. Half the wardrobe is made up of black clothing, the next dominant colour is white, then green, then it's just random bursts of orange, blue and pink. I hate all of my clothes. I stare into the fabric mess of my wardrobe and feel a tension building in the back of my head as I desperately try to choose an outfit.

BRAIN: We've got nothing to wear.

Stupidly, she's right, but it's not that I have too few clothes. If anything, I have too many, but none of them are right. They're all a mismatch of identities I have tried to don over the last ten years of my life. All these identities are usually the result of whoever I've decided looks the coolest on Instagram that week. A pair of PVC trousers and an all-frills busty bandeau? Off I head to Vinted to find something as close as possible to that outfit. The bundle of parcels arrive, and I know the delivery person is judging me for being so reckless, but in that moment I don't care. A newer, improved me is on the inside of this array of cardboard boxes. I tear the parcels open and the excitement leaves my body as I wonder why I ever thought 'gothic rave/punk' was my new aesthetic. The buyer's remorse sets in and I feel guilt wash over my body, I am a wasteful, ridiculous human who wants to kill the earth. I hate myself for it. Off my regretful purchases go to the fabric mess that is my wardrobe.

I put on outfit number one: a pair of denim jeans and a white t-shirt. Basic, simple.

BRAIN: Oh, here we go again, Little Miss Boring.

Right, fine. I did wear the same thing yesterday, and the day before. Maybe I am boring.

I try again, outfit number two: a black dress. Pretty, simple, kind of smocky.

BRAIN: My God! Are we pregnant?!

UTERUS: *gasps* It looks like we're having twins!

Seriously? Is it that unflattering? In the shop, I thought it looked nice. Modest, yes, but also sort of chic. The shop assistant said I looked great.

BRAIN: She was obviously lying, pea-head.
Burn it.

I toss the dress into the ever-growing pile on my floor that I've invisibly labelled as 'Charity Shop' but always seems to end up back in the fabric mess.

Onto the next outfit – third times a charm. I pull on a long-sleeved green midi dress I bought five years ago, and pop on a pair of ankle socks and trainers.

BOOBS: Uh, you better be joking.

I look down at the girls. They're well covered, I don't see a problem. This, if anything, is a good thing.

BOOBS: We didn't realise you were such a prude. Are you ashamed of us?

No. I mean, sometimes yes, but only because I don't want to be ogled at by random men who think it's OK to do so.

An hour later, my bedroom looks like a bomb has gone off, as I stand in my boring old white t-shirt and jeans, asking myself the same question I always do: who the fuck am I? Obviously this question goes deeper than clothes, but up until now, they've always been a good place to start. If that is what we're going off, then my wardrobe would suggest I'm a goth-punk cowboy who loves to rave, but occasionally likes to keep it super modest.

Tights and a leotard

When I was a teenager, I *knew* I was a dancer. My uniform consisted of tights and a leotard, which I would wear five days a week to train in after school. I was no good at tap dancing. I hated it. It made me think of people crushing aluminium cans, something I once saw on *Blue Peter*. I have no idea why, but the image really stayed with me, and it was all I could think about whenever I saw anyone doing that little jig. I also hated ballet. It was too disciplined and structured. Why did my hair always have to be glued to my head in a bun? Little did I know that in my later years that greasy, glued-to-my-head bun would actually be a lifesaver.

I did, however, love jazz. For a quiet kid, this was the one place I could really let loose. Energetically jumping around the room like I was the back-up dancer for Britney Spears? That was absolutely for me. I started dancing at the same time as my cousin, and as we both got closer to university age, it became clear that she was going to give being a professional dancer a serious go. I, on the other hand, had become obsessed with simply becoming Britney Spears, I didn't want to be her back-up dancer anymore. Plus a red catsuit and a live snake for a necklace – a far more reasonable dream. As I waved my cousin off to The Royal Ballet School, I hung up my tights for the final time and prepared to transform into a pop star.

A Topshop blazer

It turns out it's really hard to be a pop star. Maybe even harder than becoming a prima ballerina. But never mind, because I decided to become a broadcast journalist instead. I didn't have the voice to be a pop star, nor the stamina; talking seemed easier than singing, and I'd always enjoyed being in front of the camera. I got into a great course at university, packed my smartest shirts and most structured Topshop blazer, and headed off to set the screen on fire with . . . you know, news and stuff. Fun.

At first, everything went well. I got decent grades, some work experience, but I didn't feel great. In fact, I felt pretty sad all of the time. I began to wonder if it was because most news is bad news, and I was the one ruining everyone's day by delivering that bad news. I don't know if you've watched the news recently, but it's hell out there. Maybe once in a while you get to report that a puppy saved a kitten from a well, but 99 per cent of the time it's politics, war and grief. By the time I finished my degree, I knew it wasn't for me, but hey, at least I had a load of student debt to remind me of this chapter of my life.

Pencil skirt and flats

A bright-eyed new graduate, I was ready to enter the job market . . . and eight months later, I finally did! I was always told that once you graduate from university you have to move to London – apparently it's the place where all your dreams come true. So I moved up to London. After what felt like hundreds of rejection letters, on the day my overdraft finally maxed out, I landed a role as an intern at a beauty company. Every day, in a pencil skirt, floofy blouse and flats, I'd get to the office by 7.30am and set about answering calls and making PowerPoint presentations while trying to impress my much-cooler-than-me manager.

The problem with living in London was that no matter how much I earned, I seemed to spend more, and not even on fun things, just stepping out of the front door felt like an expense. I was so low on funds that I'd often walk two-and-a-half hours home rather than paying for the train. I then started to pick up work at a restaurant by my flat to try to make ends meet. My friends who lived only minutes away hadn't seen me for weeks. I was exhausted.

One day, almost on a whim, I decided that enough was enough. I couldn't be a slave to the 9–5 anymore. And like any other 20-something with a dream, absolutely no plan, and only the money I'd earned from tips, I packed my bags and flew to Australia on the cheapest one-way ticket I could find.

T-shirt, shorts and a backpack

I arrived by Greyhound bus on a beautiful stretch of road outside Cardwell, Australia, where I was due to start work on a banana farm. I wore an old t-shirt and thread-bare shorts, but I didn't care what I looked like. The sun was shining, my phone was off, and I'd stopped wearing make-up. The view from the road was unbelievable. It looked like it had been green-screened and I wondered how anyone ever left this place when you had that to wake up to every morning. The sea looked impossibly blue and seemed to stretch forever without a cloud in the sky – you couldn't tell where the sea ended and the sky began. By the road there was a whole species of tree I'd never seen before and every area was filled with brightly coloured flowers.

Every day, I'd pack bananas into boxes, before stuffing bananas into my mouth for breakfast, lunch and dinner. On Friday nights, we'd head over to the one local pub, get absolutely wankered, and spend Saturday at a local water-fall jumping off rocks into the most gorgeous, clear water. I also got to drive a tractor around the banana paddocks and that felt like I had won the lottery. Yet as much as I loved being a banana farmer, all good things must come to an end, as a new job offer had come through.

100 per cent polyester

Next was that brand-new job in a brand-new country. But because I was a barmaid in the British pub at Epcot, the international theme park at Disney World, Florida, it felt like several countries all at once but also none at all. I was dressed head to toe in polyester in an outfit that I can only describe as 'wench': a pink skirt, criss-crossed bodice and puffy sleeve, complete with a massive burgundy skirt and cream half-apron.

I was living in employee housing and working 60 to 70 hours a week, but having an amazing time. Partly because I was so disconnected from real life that it was like I'd been plonked onto the set of a film. While my London friends were trudging to work, I was watching fireworks, eating burgers, riding rollercoasters and posting smug captions on my Instagram like: 'I can't believe I get to live here ;)'. I'd become *that* person and apparently I didn't even care.

Pyjamas

Then Covid-19 hit and I left The Happiest Place On Earth to return to the Isle of Wight. Back home, I had no idea who I was, and without the excuse to wear my shabbiest farming shorts or the crutch of a wench uniform, I could barely bring myself to get dressed.

With no job, no prospects and no plan, I began making short comedy videos and uploading them to my YouTube channel. People (my mum, dad and grandma) seemed to like them, so I kept going. I sat down and wrote out everything I wanted to manifest in my life from this point onwards.

- I want a career that I enjoy
- I want to work in comedy
- I want to reach a million followers online
- I want to own a house
- I want to be happy
- I want to live somewhere I enjoy living

Over the next few months, my social media following grew and grew. By April 2021, it was my full-time job. I wasn't just wearing my pyjamas, as I was now making comedy sketches where I had conversations with my body every day. I'd be dressed up as my brain, a vulva and even a hairy nipple. I started to wake up every single day feeling so full of joy and gratitude and excitement. How lucky was I to be dressed as a pube?

*

My mum once said to me, 'What is meant for you will not pass you by.' At the moments in my life when I've felt most unsure about who I am, or what I'm supposed to be doing, I lean on these words. Knowing what you want to do with your life does not define you, but when you find something that sparks joy and gets you excited, persevere with that thing and follow where it leads.

Most of all, I know that finding yourself takes time. So today, standing in front of the mirror in my white t-shirt and jeans once again, I'm going to give myself a break. Basic and simple. It's not who I am, but it works for now.

Weird Lies I Told about
My Rabbit

When I was in Year 5, my best friend (who was also called Hayley) had a dog called Dave. It was an odd name for such a cute dog, but I figured they'd probably named it after a dead relative, or their favourite binman. He was a Shih Tzu by name, Shih Tzu by nature, but I was still incredibly jealous that they had Dave. All day long, Hayley would brag about how Dave could do all kinds of tricks – roll over, beg for a treat, bark on cue, fetch the newspaper. These are all relatively normal dog things, but in my mind that little hairy guy was some kind of dog genius. I was livid.

I spent months doing my own begging (I didn't need any treats), but my parents refused to get me a dog. It was so unfair – just because my dad had grown up with 13 Great Danes and my mum with one very hyperactive dog, it meant that they were all 'dogged out'. It was a hard thing to accept but, months later, we finally compromised by getting a rabbit called Charlie. Determined to test the limits of Charlie's amazing mind powers, I created a dedicated learning centre for him, filled with toys, games and tiny challenges. Sadly, he was rubbish at all of them, so I decided I'd just have to make some stuff up. After all, I couldn't let Hayley continue to go on about her magical pet-owner powers, when I clearly had a rabbit genius on my hands. Here are a few of the lies I told.

My rabbit watches television

What is 'watching' anyway, except being pointed in the direction of something while owning eyes? I would sit Charlie on my lap to watch *CITV* every Saturday morning, so in a way he was watching it too. I'd also say he'd pick out programmes in the *Radio Times* by pooping on the listing he wanted, which was technically true, because the pages all ended up in his hutch. Maybe he was just a slow learner?

My rabbit can tightrope walk

I've always dreamed of being able to do circus tricks, but I once landed on my neck doing a forward roll on a trampoline and swore off that idea for life. Charlie, however, was pretty good at circus stunts, like getting in and out of his bed on the little ramp that we built him. And what is a ramp, I ask you, but a chunky tightrope? Exactly. My rabbit was way more talented than stupid Dave.

My rabbit can read minds

I'm not saying that Charlie could see the future, but if it was going to rain – or had already started to rain just a little bit – he would head back inside his hutch almost immediately. Also, when I was feeling sad, he'd come and sit in my lap (because I put him there). Dave was too stupid to even realise it was pouring with rain; Dave always smelled like wet dog.

My rabbit saved us from a house fire

This sounds dramatic, doesn't it? When I told my friends that my house was burning to the ground when Charlie shuffled in and dragged me to safety, they gasped audibly at the image of my tiny rabbit saving my life. What actually happened was that my mum knocked over a candle and Charlie stamped his foot very loudly before biting my finger. Thankfully I lived so far away from my school that my friends never came back to my house for dinner, so they couldn't verify this.

My rabbit sleeps on my bed with me

He wasn't supposed to get on my bed – that's definitely just meant to be a dog thing. But I still gave it a good go, although he always escaped in the middle of the night. This is an attitude I've employed with men ever since. Still, just like rabbits they also have a habit of escaping in the middle of the night.

Ten Weird Things that Everyone Does (and if You Don't, You Should)

I used to assume I was a little freak because I was always up to really weird things – conversations with myself, routines, rituals and games – that no one else seemed to do. Perhaps there's something wrong with me, I thought. Eventually, after a lot of thinking, I realised that there are almost eight billion people on earth, and surely we're mostly doing the same things as each other . . . We are all human after all.

1. Practice fake arguments in the shower

If you're not having an imaginary fight at least once a month, who are you, and why don't you crave the taste of drama? The older I get, the fewer real arguments I seem to have, so in the shower I fill my time with fantasy arguments with mythical boyfriends, dead celebrities, and friends from school that I haven't seen in more than a decade. Sometimes I practise arguments I might have in the future, or I go back over past disputes, now armed with the greatest comebacks you've ever heard. Why can I never think of these in real time? By the time I step onto the shower mat, my shampoo bottle is a quivering mess.

2. Pretend not to notice someone who is walking directly towards you until they are standing right in front of you

It's nice to meet up with friends at a planned time and place after months of organising. What's less nice is the incredibly long period between when you first spot someone in the distance, and when you're finally close enough to interact with them. If you make eye contact too soon, you risk having to smile and wave for what feels like half a mile. Instead, you fumble around with your phone, opening and closing apps to make it look like you're doing something really absorbing, right up until they reach you. Then you have to act really surprised that they've suddenly appeared out of nowhere. Sometimes I throw in an, 'Oh, there you are, I'm not wearing my glasses!' for good measure, even though I don't wear glasses and we both know it.

3. Talk to yourself in the mirror when you're drunk

You're in the pub, six drinks and two shots deep. You slink off to the toilets. It's a closed cubical, complete with a sink and mirror. As you wash your hands, you catch sight of your very own drunk twin. 'You're doing great,' you mutter, 'you're not too drunk and everyone likes you'. 'Thanks, me,' you reply, 'I'll see you in an hour! Don't do anything I wouldn't do!'

4. Think about your own funeral

Thinking about death? Bad, dark, very depressing. Imagining your funeral? Moving, thrilling, and dare I say it, exciting. Will the guy you fancy be there? Will he cry? Will he make a speech? You wonder what photo they'll choose for the order of service, and vow to take a flattering shot at least once a month from now on. What songs will they play? You scroll through your Spotify. Time to make a playlist. I do not want to be remembered as the girl who exclusively listened to songs from 2002's *Fame Academy*.

5. Take pictures of yourself crying

Look, I can't explain it, but I think I look absolutely gorgeous when I cry and I don't say that lightly. Those little wet eyes coupled with a perfectly pink nose? I've never looked so good. I mean, damn, misery looks fabulous on me. Photoshoot coming up? Time to whack on *Marley and Me*.

6. Wonder if you're in *The Truman Show*

I first watched *The Truman Show* – a film about a man who is raised inside a fictional world built for a TV show, but doesn't know he's being watched by a huge audience – when I was eight years old. From that moment, I was certain that it was about me. After all, how would you know?

Everyone was conspiring to make him feel like he was living in reality, so how could I be sure they weren't doing the same to me? Plus, I'm absolutely fascinating, obviously. It would be a waste if there *wasn't* an audience watching my every move. I can just imagine them gasping, 'Look, she's in the supermarket again! Maybe later she'll fall asleep during a film!' A truly riveting watch for everyone.

7. Check if a 'certain someone' has watched your Instagram story

The whole point of Instagram stories is to see who fancies you and who hates you. There, I've said it. I'm not trying to imply that everyone who watches your story is either desperately in love with you or wants the worst for you. Lots of people are just chronically online or went to primary school with your cousin or whatever. No, I'm talking about the cutie you're uploading the photo *for*. As soon as you press send, it's impossible to resist checking whether they've seen it. Over and over again. If you ever want to let someone know you're not interested, just stop looking at their Instagram stories and they'll be firmly informed. If we're dating and you look at my stories on the regular? We're getting married immediately. I'll also make sure to watch my own story back with their POV in mind, just to get a taste of how they see me.

8. Picture how random couples have sex

You're walking along, minding your own business, when you spot a couple. They're not kissing or fighting or doing anything strange at all, but suddenly Brain pops up to ask you what you think they look like when they have sex. Is she on top? Is he? Do they try out different positions? Do they go all night long, or is it more of an afternoon delight? Maybe they're a vanilla kind of couple? You definitely don't fancy them, you're also not sure why you're wondering this. In fact, you'll never think of them again, but in that moment you were more a part of their life than they'll ever know.

9. Sniff a new book

I love crack, by which I mean the crack between the pages of a brand-new book. I sneak around bookshops like a junkie, taking huge, huffing gulps of that fresh book smell. My God, there really is nothing like it. Libraries aren't so bad either, they're just a little mustier, occasionally contain mystery crumbs, and you look a bit more seedy doing it in there. It really is the brothel of book-based venues. But new books . . . Don't believe me? Give it a try! You get one free sniff of this book on me.

10. Imagine how you'd survive a zombie
    apocalypse

The world is a scary place, and it's getting more terrifying by the day. I don't know about you, but I can barely tell the difference between reality and television anymore. Seriously, all my memories have been replaced with *Love Island* and *Keeping Up With the Kardashians*, everything I see I'm consumed by and I don't know what real life is. Because of this, I spend quite a lot of time thinking through my strategy for surviving a zombie attack. Would I fight? Would I hide? Would I eat a dog if I absolutely had to? Better buy a couple of extra cans of baked beans, just in case.

Brain vs Puberty

Sometimes people younger than me ask me for advice. This is fine when it comes to low-rise jeans (they may be back in fashion but avoid at all costs – they look bad in photos, although on the plus side they do make eating out easier without all that fabric pushing on your stomach) or dating much older guys (they may be back in fashion but avoid at all costs – they look bad in photos, although on the plus side they do make eating out easier because they pay for everything), but there is one thing that under no circumstances can I claim to be an expert in: puberty. Because I handled puberty like I was completely unhinged.

The thing about puberty is that one minute you and your friends are all exactly the same cartoon-watching children that love playing with Bratz dolls, and then the next minute Sarah is buying her first bra while you're still watching *Looney Tunes* with Sasha (your favourite of the Bratz).

School is full of weird, random pressures. You want

to be cool, but not talked about, good at exams, but not in a try-hard way. To study before a test was probably the least cool thing you could do, but failing wouldn't get you any brownie points either, so you had to pretend you weren't doing any revision and then just casually ace the exam like it was no big deal. At my school (and this'll very clearly mark my age) your popularity was measured by your MySpace Top 8 – a visible ranking of your favourite people, friends or otherwise. If you weren't in the top four of at least six people's MySpace Top 8, you were a certified freak and no one wanted to talk to you.

As soon as my friends started going through puberty, I began to worry about how underdeveloped I was. So, like two kids in a trench coat sneaking into the cinema, I decided to commit extra hard to pretending I was an adult. Sadly, I fooled absolutely no one, because I looked like I was eight right up until the day of my 16th birthday.

The changing rooms at school were always hell. At the time, I had an especially interesting outie belly button; it was a quirk of mine that I'd never really given much thought to before I reached school. It stuck out quite a bit and slightly flopped downwards, and of course, like any self-conscious kid at school, I was always worried about it. I avoided two-piece bathing suits and always, always wore a tightly tucked in vest under my school uniform so that there was no chance of anyone seeing it. Ever. But before PE one day, when my class was in the changing rooms, one of the girls noticed it as my vest slid up my stomach. She then announced to the class that I had a willy on my stomach. Everyone looked at me and ogled. A few months later, after crying every day to my parents about how much I hated my tummy, I had my belly button re-stitched so it became an innie. One of the kids a few years below me punched me in the stitches and asked me if it hurt to be kicked in the willy. It did hurt, a lot.

My school was ruled by the popular girls. They were pretty, slight, all wore thongs with matching padded bras, apparently lost their virginity by 15 and, of course, every boy at school fancied them. I had none of these things, but at least I now had an innie belly button. At 14 I still hadn't even started my period. This was my deepest, darkest secret, because as far as my friends knew, I'd been bleeding almost continuously for about three years.

In Year 7, my two closest friends were Lauren and Jennifer. We did everything together. Our favourite pastime was chatting, which we did during lessons, during break time and after school on MSN. Chatting is to pre-teen girls what watching sports is to pre-teen boys – just an excuse to talk about hot, sweaty bodies.

Lauren, Jennifer and I were three peas in a pod – if two of those peas had boobs, and one was just a regular, flat-chested pea. They were both probably a foot taller than me, looked at least three school years older and, by 11, were hitting puberty hard. At our sleepovers, they would talk about what it was like to buy bras, while I nodded along, having absolutely no idea what it was like to even wear a bra, let alone buy one. The only experience

I had with bras was holding my mum's onto my face like it was a pair of alien eyes and running round the house trying to scare my family.

Just as she turned 12, Jennifer burst into our registration class with big news. 'I've started my period!'

I could see she was thrilled. I wasn't. Fear, panic and jealousy washed over me. Now it was just me and Lauren, the two musketeers. Just two period-less peas in a pod. A few weeks later, Lauren had to leave English because she had a tummy ache. I knew what that meant even before she did, Jennifer had told us about these tummy aches she'd get before her period came. I watched as Jennifer and Lauren exchanged pads and hugs at lunchtime, while I was all alone, one single, flat-chested pea in my period-less pod.

After that, I spent my school days like a wistful 1930s woman, staring out of the window, waiting for her husband to return from war. Except my husband was my period, and war was the feeling of, 'When the hell is my period going to get here? And why do I still look like I'm eight?'

PERIOD: My God! You are so desperate, it's sickening. At least play it a bit cool. It's me who calls the shots, not you. Think you know me? You don't know me.

A few months later, we were hanging out in the quiet toilets at the back of the school that no one ever went to. I don't know why, but every school seems to have these, and everyone claims to have hung out in them, and yet they were always totally empty. On this day, Jennifer had her period and was browsing a cornucopia of pads and tampons in Lauren's cute little zip bag. Everything looked so bright and colourful that I wanted to be choosing a bright green, flowery pad from Lauren's bag too. Suddenly, I felt the most overwhelming wave of FOMO. I just wanted to know what it was like.

BRAIN: Say we've started our period.

No! I can't lie! What a weird thing to lie about. Plus, they'll know, they'll obviously know. They're basically experts in bleeding.

BRAIN: How would they know?

Brain's words echoed around my head. Could I? Should I? Would I? Who would it hurt? I don't think anyone's ever hurt anyone by saying they've started their period.

Except when Lauren told me. That was the worst day of my life. Actually, getting called 'willy girl' might have been worse than that. And in fairness, I'd almost certainly be starting my period soon anyway, surely? So it would only be a half-lie. It could start tomorrow for all I know. Before I could think anymore, I heard myself blurting out, 'I've got my period!'

The girls paused and looked at me, eyes narrowed. My body started sweating profusely, my eyes were going

AWOL all over the room. I could see the disbelief on their faces. This was so stupid. Why would I have waited until the end of lunchtime to bring up this meteoric news? And what were the chances I would have come on at the exact same time as Jennifer?

PERIOD: God, you really are new to this, aren't you?! Obviously, it could happen, I freaking live to randomly sync up with your friends. Oh, you live together, do you? Get ready for pure chaos for a whole week. What a way to test a friendship – I am all over this kind of drama.

Suddenly, Jennifer donned an invisible sequin blazer and went into full quizmaster mode. 'Tampons or pads?'

BRAIN: Isn't it just the girls who've lost their virginities that are using tampons? Phone a friend.

'Pads.'
    'Heavy or light?'

BRAIN: What does that even mean? It's a 50/50 answer . . . go with heavy.

'Heavy.'
    'When did you come on?'
    I froze. This felt like it needed some detail – some flavour and pizazz to really bring the story to life.

BRAIN: Ooh! I know! Say it started in the shower, and the water went bright red like in that horror film we watched 15 minutes of one night and got so scared we couldn't sleep.

And like a tiny, blonde, eight-year-old Alfred Hitchcock, I described the scene of graphic horror in all its gory detail. I thought I'd taken it a step too far when I told them blood was raining from the ceiling, but it felt like the right thing to add. Jennifer and Lauren's faces fell. They didn't say anything for a while. I wondered whether I should continue, add a few more gory details. Something about a severed finger?

At last, Lauren spoke: 'Prove it.'

BRAIN: Oh brilliant. Someone didn't think this through, did they? Now we're stuffed. I told you not to lie. What a ridiculous thing to lie about.

'I . . . I . . .'

The school bell rang. I was saved! I scuttled off to class. A class that neither of them were in. Phew.

At the end of the day, I ran straight home and tried not to think about my lie. That is, until I opened MSN messenger. Jennifer and Lauren agreed that if I wanted to stay friends with them, I'd have to prove I'd got my period. I saw my name had already been removed from their MSN screen names and a pit formed in my stomach. The Three Amigos, the three peas in a pod, they'd be no more. I knew I'd have to come clean.

BRAIN: Unless . . .

A genius idea. I ran to my bedroom and dug out one of the period pads my mum had bought me just in case. Now I just needed some blood. I remembered my brother had some fake blood capsules left over from Halloween, so I snuck into his room like Tom Cruise in *Mission Impossible*, but without any of the ropes. Or the gadgets. OK, I just walked into his room, but I tried not to touch anything, because I didn't want to have to explain myself to him. It wouldn't end well if he knew I was in there – we were way too protective over our bedrooms – plus having to talk to him about periods? No thanks.

PERIOD: Wow. Seriously? Ashamed of me already. You do realise men need to know about periods too?

It's not my problem right now.

There, in the drawer next to his bed, were the capsules. Bingo!

I headed straight for the bathroom and peeled the pad off its backing. It smelled suspiciously like hospitals. I had a plan. This white-as-snow pad wouldn't be white for much longer. I splayed the pad out on the worktop, bit the top off the capsule, and spread the bright red blood over every inch of it. This wasn't just a heavy period, this was a massacre.

BRAIN: Wait, periods do look like massacres, right? Blood does rain from the ceiling?

I may not have had much of a sex education, but I was positive it was every bit as dramatic as I'd imagined. I popped the pad into a ziplock bag and slid it into my school bag. All night I dreamed about big, red tidal waves, big, red slip-and-slides, big, angry, red monsters . . .

BRAIN: . . . and the dragon from *Shrek* feeding you grapes.

Woah! That's private!

The next day, at the appointed time, we gathered in the empty toilets. I told the girls to go into the cubicle next to me. I needed to remove the pad from its ziplock bag and stick it on the gusset of my knickers so it looked really convincing.

As soon as I was done setting the scene, I told them to look over the top of the cubicle. There they were, peering over like two giants, as I crouched on my tiny porcelain throne. Jennifer and Lauren gasped as they saw the pad. They believed me and, my God, they were impressed. I felt amazing, like one of the gang again. I was back in the pod and I didn't ever want that feeling to end.

My friendship with Lauren and Jennifer fizzled out as they got boyfriends. None of the boys at my school fancied me, because I still looked so much younger than all the other girls. I was with my new friends now. Who had somehow heard I'd already started my period. So, for the next three years, I wore a pad every single day. I waddled around school like an adult baby, hoping and praying that my period would begin. Whenever it happened, I would be ready for it, and until then, I'd lie.

Whenever anyone asked, I was on my period – three times a month if necessary. No one bled more than me. I began to stuff my bra, portraying a fake puberty that was perfect down to the smallest detail. I became competitive. My friend Kimberley and I would phone each other after school to recount the number of pubes we had. If she had four, I'd say five, looking down at my completely hairless body.

One day, I was sitting in the school loos when I looked down and noticed that not only had a single stray pube formed (oh my God), but also that my pad actually did have the smallest smear of very dark brown blood on it. And when I wiped, there was more. This was it! Finally! My period had started! I'd hit puberty! I was a full-blown adult! I wanted to scream and shout, except . . . I couldn't tell anyone. Because of my stupid lies, I now had a new secret, and this one was even harder to keep.

When my tiny boobs finally came in, I was in the unique position of having to unstuff my bra a little bit every day, just to try and keep them the same size. I had to act like I was very body conscious as my friends would compare boob sizes at sleepovers while I kept all my clothes on. I even slept in a bra.

About a year in, I realised my real boobs were never

going to make it to their aspirational proportions, so I began saving my pocket money for a boob job. Little did I know, my £15 a month allowance would mean I'd be saving for at least 33 years to even get close to being able to afford one. Turns out, being part of the itty bitty titty committee as an adult is actually pretty great. I used the money to buy myself a massive 18-inch TV.

So if you ever ask for my advice about puberty, here's what I'll say: don't lie.

But if you must, just say you're using tampons.

Me vs Period

Once my period arrived for real, she couldn't stop show-ing up suddenly at the worst possible times. She was right, I really was never going to be able to control her. In those first few years her visits still weren't regular or predictable, and I always felt completely ambushed, like she was constantly waiting behind my bush to jump out and scare me.

About six months after Period first checked into the Uterus Hotel ('Spacious, 4 stars, better than expected' – TripAdvisor), I was invited on my first ever holiday with my new best friend Immy. It was supposed to be just me, Immy and her mum, but as the trip approached, and with no sign of Period for several weeks, I began to worry that she would invite herself along.

PERIOD: This is how it works! You tell me whatever the most inconvenient time for you is, and I'll be there! You can count on it. I long to make your life a misery.

Up to this point I'd still been working through the back-log of massive pads my mum had bought me, that I was beyond embarrassed about her buying years before I even started. For some reason, 'becoming a woman', though I was desperate for it to happen, was also the most embar-rassing thing for me.

As Immy and I set about our holiday plans and began running through our water park strategy, I knew that these pads simply weren't going to cut it under a bikini. One waterslide in and I'd be dragging around an extra 30 pounds of liquid in my gusset. It was finally time to try tampons – much to my dismay. After all, I still believed that tampons could only be used once you had been 'deflowered'.

I stuffed my suitcase with teen-girl holiday essentials – highly carcinogenic hairspray, a backcombing brush, nine books, sticky lip gloss, a crumbling eyeshadow palette, my very toxic Britney Spears perfume, and one box of Lil-lets – and headed off on holiday, ready to look at some boys from across a teen nightclub before never, ever talk-ing to them.

On day three, Period – as I suspected she might – came knocking.

PERIOD: Oh hey! Looks like you're having a good time in that lovely white skirt of yours. Feeling relaxed, are we? How would you like some stomach pains and a brand new stain . . . of course I won't let you answer that. Surprise, I'm here!

It was time. I headed back to my room and tentatively opened the box of Lil-lets. They looked like tiny, unmenacing bullets.

I suddenly realised I had absolutely no idea how tampons worked. I knew they went . . . inside, but . . . how? And where? I locked myself in the bathroom and spent almost an hour trying to work it out. It was an unsolvable puzzle, one of the great mysteries, like, 'Who built the pyramids?' or 'Why are women's razors more expensive than men's even though they're exactly the same but seem to remove only half the hair?'

I contorted my body like an Olympic gymnast, throwing my legs over my head in ways I'd never even thought possible. I hit my head repeatedly on the sink. I laughed, I screamed, I cried. I missed dinner. But I couldn't get it in. Of course, I didn't even think to ask Immy or her mum for help. Her mum was a midwife, she'd know exactly how to do it. That would have been too easy.

So it was back to the massive pads. Since I couldn't go on the waterslides while wearing them, my only option was to forgo swimming, skip the fun, and sit on a towel while wearing shorts for the rest of the holiday. I'm not sure her mum believed me when I told her that it was because watching *Titanic* had made me change my views on large bodies of water.

Once home, I was determined to get to grips with tampons. Aside from ruining my trip, pads made me walk like a cowboy, and your body, your choice, but I personally think there's something really off-putting about being able to feel your uterus lining leave your body. But that's just me being a squeamish freak who passes out at the sight of anything too gory. On a one-woman mission, I went incognito (I put on sunglasses) to my local pharmacy, where I could survey the enemy and consider my options in peace.

That's when I first discovered that some tampons came with applicators. What a revelation, how did I not know about this before? Yes! I bought a couple of packs, smuggled them home, and set to work reading the instructions. All of the instructions. Pages and pages, in a tiny book with a tiny font, presumably for dolls to read. And just as I was ready to give up and slide that tampon into my vagina like a push-up lolly, I saw it: 'Symptoms of Toxic Shock Syndrome (TSS) may include fever, diarrhoea, vomiting, fainting, dizziness or a rash.'

Right on cue, Brain came rushing in.

BRAIN: There's no way you're poking that thing up our fanny. Do you want us to die?

It can't be that likely, I thought. Millions of people use tampons every day, and how many of them are dead?

BRAIN: It might be rare, but if it's life-threatening, let's be honest, it's going to happen to us. We're always unlucky.

I tried to think back over all the times I'd forgotten to

do normal, everyday things like changing a tampon . . . but I couldn't remember any! A bad sign indeed. Plus, Brain was right, dying of an easily preventable condition is exactly the kind of thing that would happen to me. How embarrassing, for everyone at your funeral to know you passed away at 17 from *checks notes* the contents of your own vagina. What a mad thing for my grandparents to have to find out.

I was now a tampon user, petrified every cycle that I was hours from death. I'd insert a tampon and every symptom of my period would seem like a symptom of TSS. Every few hours I'd change it, always worried I'd forget one was in there and accidentally insert another. I heard so many horror stories.

At a family friend's wedding, myself and my three best friends took advantage of the free bar. We were doing shot after shot until Jess started throwing up over the back patio of the venue. So the four of us got a cab back to Jess's place to put her to bed. She was coated in her own sick, so of course, like the good friends we were, we decided to pop her in the shower. Once we got her out of the shower and onto the floor, we remembered Jess was on her period and had been wearing a tampon since 10am.

It was now 9pm.

BRAIN: Oh my God! TSS! She's going to die and it's on your watch!

Brain was right, it was hours past the recommended

amount of time you should have a tampon in for. I'd been doing no more than three hours as a precaution, so this seemed potentially fatal. The three of us did rock, paper, scissors to see who would be the one to have to remove Jess's tampon.

Given my luck, I should have known it was going to be me. Jess was passed out on the floor of the bathroom where we'd dropped her after getting her out of the shower. She was a complete deadweight and far too heavy for three very drunk girls. I pulled out her tampon and flung it towards the bin, missing and hitting the mirror. That was the day I saved a life, and swore off tampons for good.

A quick Google search a month later led me to menstrual cups. They weren't new, but no one I knew was using one, so I felt like an intrepid explorer. I picked a brand based on four good reviews that seemed legit and not from paid-for bots. After guessing whether I had a high cervix, a low cervix or a medium cervix – a real Goldilocks situation – I made my purchase.

The cup arrived two days later, and I was strangely excited about trying it out. I started watching YouTube videos about how to insert and, more importantly, remove it, and was feeling really good about my choices. When my period finally arrived, I was ready and raring to go.

I grabbed the cup and some lube, and after a few haphazard attempts, I was in! Several hours went by, which I passed watching TV and feeling smug, because TSS wasn't as much of a risk now, and I was also basically saving the planet. At last it was time to fish it out for a refresh. Simple.

I went to the bathroom, locked the door and sat on the toilet, legs spread. I hooked my index finger inside, feeling for the little stem that helps you pull it out.

It wasn't there. What the hell? Where had it gone?

BRAIN: Maybe it fell out somewhere and you didn't notice.

How? I'd been wearing trousers this entire time. Surely I'd have seen a bloody cup falling out of my vagina?

I grabbed a mirror and tried to peer up inside myself, looking for any sign at all of the cup. By this point, I'd started to vividly imagine the ambulance coming to pick me up and take me to hospital, where a doctor would break the bad news: 'You are part woman, part cup forever now.'

Suddenly, after really angling my body, I spotted it! Well, I could just about see it, but I couldn't wriggle it loose. At least not while sitting on the toilet. Flashing back to my holiday tampon adventure, I lay down on the floor, legs on the edge of the bath, and prayed. I was desperate for this little silicone wine goblet to leave my body.

Pushing like I was giving birth, I tore that bloody cup out of me, spraying menses across the wall, and crying out in triumph. It's a miracle! A whole fucking miracle! I am so powerful, I am—

'Is everything alright in there, Hayley?'

—going to have to clean this mess up before my mum sees it.

The happy ending of this story was that I grew to love my menstrual cup. I might even go so far as to say it's my favourite possession. I enjoy that you get to act like a chef, because every time you use it you have to boil it in a pan. It's like bobbing for apples, except you don't use your mouth and it's boiling-hot water. I've now properly mastered the art of inserting and removing it: little tip, bear down like you're about to pop out an intimidatingly large poop, breathe a sigh of relief and there it is, your baby cup.

UTERUS: Now you're fully trained we can push out an actual baby!

Absolutely not the same thing.

Fictional Characters I've Fancied

There's nothing more exciting than having a crush on someone. That heart-racing, weak-at-the-knees feeling that lets you know you're alive. When I fancy someone, they're the only thing I can think about from morning to night – forget about anything else I'm supposed to be doing, it's all about romanticising my life with that person. Especially if there's no chance we'll ever get together, which was especially true when I was a kid and pretty much all of my crushes were on fictional characters. That's when the crush becomes all-consuming. For now I mostly fancy real people – in fact it's usually people I actually know. And though I've moved on from my childhood crushes, I still look back on all of them with great fondness.

Age 5: If I'd had three wishes, I'd have used all of them to hang out with Aladdin. The purple waistcoat? The baggy trousers? And a pet monkey? I wanted us to fly off on my Early Learning Centre carpet to a whole new world. What a dreamboat.

Age 6: He's the king of the jungle and the prince of my heart — that's right, let's hear a roar for Simba. I didn't realise then that human/lion relationships rarely work out; I just really wanted to go to the zoo all the time. Of course I knew Simba wasn't there, I just wanted to feel closer to him.

Age 7: Everyone loves a bad boy and I loved cartoon Peter Pan. With his little hat, his pointy shoes and his kind of weird views on women and homemaking, I swore we'd never grow up together.

Age 8: Enough of boys/cartoon animals, I wanted a man, and Robbie Williams was my guy. Down the water-fall, wherever it may take me, I know that . . . I'm loving Robbie instead. I secretly stuck a poster of him on the back of my door, behind my mounds of dressing gowns like a tiny pervert, and would sing his songs as I fell asleep.

Age 9: They made a live-action Peter Pan so I fancied him again. He was still a cheeky little chappie, with really swooshy blonde locks. I wonder if I have finally grown out of crushing on cartoons.

Age 10: Lemar came third in *Fame Academy* but was the undisputed winner of my heart. I was certain he was going to become one of the biggest stars in the world, and I would be his girlfriend, carrying his microphones and cheering him on from the side of the stage. He's the sole reason I got the *Fame Academy* CD for Christmas in this year.

Age 11: Get in loser, because I've just seen *Mean Girls* and I'm obsessed with Aaron Samuels. According to The Plastics he's one of the hottest and most popular guys at North Shore High School, and I agree. Also his hair looked so sexy pushed back.

Age 12: It turns out I do still fancy cartoons . . . if they're fish-shaped. That's right, I got the hots for Nemo's dad. Sure, he might be a clownfish, but he's a real daddy, plus people always tell me orange looks good on me.

Age 13: I watch *10 Things I Hate About You* and immediately find 10 things I love about Heath Ledger. I spend so long thinking about his hair that I barely notice I've watched an entire Shakespeare play without complaining.

Age 14: I was McLovin' Seth from *Superbad*, aka Jonah Hill. I was drawing dicks all over my journal, hoping he'd notice me. He was the sweetest guy – every time I looked into his eyes it felt like the first time I heard The Beatles.

Age 15: For the first time, I have an almost-age-appropriate crush (he was only three years older, the perfect age), as I fall head over heels for Alex Pettyfer. I watch *Wild Child* every single day for a year, thinking about how we might one day meet at a Hollywood party – if for some reason they randomly decided to hold one on the Isle of Wight and 15-year-olds were invited.

Age 16: Chad. Michael. Murray. *One Tree Hill* started on Channel 4 and I knew that Chad Michael Murray, aka Lucas Scott, was the one. At last, I'd found him. Every single notebook I owned was scribbled with his name and mine, together forever. I printed out pictures of him and would kiss his face before we went to bed. I thought about how we would meet at a fan event, and the world would stand still as he'd lunge in to kiss me in front of everyone. One month later, we'd get married and I'd be Mrs Hayley Michael Murray.

Age 17: Started dating real boys. Found out Chad Michael Murray is 12 years older than me. Never fancied a cartoon again . . . Until they re-made *The Lion King* and I saw Simba in his full CGI glory.

Brain vs Lungs

We've all heard about the benefits of exercise. It's drummed into us year after year. In fact, every New Year we're told that exercise is the only way to step into a brand-new you.

BRAIN: No! Not this again. Look, we tried, we turned red, our butt got sweaty and we failed. Get back on the sofa, turn on Netflix and just stop being silly.

Come on, you know the only reason you don't like it is because it forces you to shut up for a second and you can't handle being silenced.

BRAIN: Too right. I can't think under these conditions. Why does everything hurt? What are we running *from*? That's the real question we should be asking ourselves, over and over and over again.

The idea of exercise definitely appeals to me. Calm Brain down and get a super-hot bod in the process? Sounds like a win/win situation.

The main issue with exercise is, of course, that people who gush to you about the power of endorphins, the sense of achievement and how many friends they made at netball club, are usually incredibly athletic to begin with. They just strut their way onto the court, or the track, or the open road, or basically anywhere for that matter, and immediately feel amazing, without six to nine months of huffing, puffing and having to stop to loudly retch after walking for nine minutes on a very slow treadmill. Which is no way to either feel good or make new friends, and certainly doesn't leave me with the sense of achievement I am seeking.

I'm good at many things – procrastinating, mixing drinks, making my bed (alone) and panicking about stuff – but sporting activities are not really where I thrive. To be honest, over the years, exercise has probably added more stress than it's taken away, so I've learned to mostly avoid it.

BRAIN: Oh, yeah . . . What was that thing you used to do in primary school?

Wait too long to ask the teacher to go to the toilet and piss myself in art class?

BRAIN: No, not that. Though we can bank that for the next time you need to feel extremely embarrassed in a completely unrelated situation.

Oh . . . you mean the nosebleeds? Right. Yes. Nosebleeds.

When I was in primary school, every Friday we'd be trotted out in a tiny human train in our fluorescent safety vests to our local swimming pool for—

BRAIN: Ritual humiliation.

Swimming lessons. A boy in my class called Luke Balding and I would always head straight down to the deep end, where we'd take it in turns to 'accidentally' belly flop into the water to see who could get a nosebleed first. It's not an Olympic sport, sure, but we liked it, and we were good at it. It was mainly because having a nosebleed would mean we were immediately exempt from any further swimming activities that day. Plus we'd get unlimited attention from the rest of the class. Now that's a real win/win situation.

I know what you're thinking: nosebleeds? On cue? You must have been really popular at school. And you'd be right – it was always a hot girl thing to have a nosebleed. I can't explain the logic of children, but if nosebleeds were modelling jobs, I was the bloody Kate Moss of Year 3. However, my plan soon hit a roadblock when my parents insisted I had both nostrils cauterised. I had no idea what this entailed. It sounded to me like I was going to have my nostrils sewn together or chopped off completely.

I was taken to a building that I'd never been to before. The corridor leading down to the waiting room was long and dark. It felt like a scene from a horror film that I'm sure I wouldn't have liked the ending of. When my name was called, I was taken into an even darker and scarier-looking room where a light was shone in my face and my nose was, to put it bluntly, set on fire. I left that day feeling like something important had been stolen from me (my nostril hairs). Swimming was never interrupted again, and just like that, my hot girl/nosebleed era was over. I wept for days.

> BRAIN: I bet if we tried hard enough we could get into nosebleeds again. I reckon if we just gave our nostrils a good poke we'd get there.

Sadly, it later turned out I was quite a good swimmer. I wasn't the best in my class of course, maybe because my outie belly button was weighing me down. Once I'd successfully completed all my proficiencies, I went on to swim a mile, and then, for some reason completely unbeknown to me, two miles. On the plus side, I did end up earning a handful of Kellogg's badges that my mum refused to sew on my swimsuit.

As I bobbed below the surface during those swimming lessons, I watched Luke Balding gushing from the nostrils, relishing in all the extra attention he got for being the last man standing (on the side of the pool, well back from the water). I refused to give him the satisfaction of asking if he was OK.

Sadly, these early setbacks meant I could never quite reach the top of the sport. The other kids in my class were way ahead of me, and now my swimming is mostly contained to short swims in the sea. That is after I've gotten over the yelping as the cold water hits me around my midriff. I'll then pad about for five minutes before convincing myself there's a shark coming and run out screaming.

> BRAIN: Look, we all saw *Jaws*. You can never be
> too safe.

However, it wasn't just water-based sports that I struggled to participate in. I was the first girl born into my dad's side of the family and, as my grandpa had only ever experienced raising boys, he was excited to show me the ropes of some of his favourite things – all of which were (of course) sports. He was desperate for me to play tennis and golf with him. We'd go out into the garden every weekend and set up my very own tiny driving range. My grandmother would watch from the kitchen window as I'd swing my little club over and over, while the ball very much remained on its tee. This is when I first learned that balls and I do not go together.

> BRAIN: That's what she said.

I'm looking back at my childhood, please get your head out of the gutter.

My grandpa was so devastated to learn that I was physically unable to swing a golf club correctly that he never spoke to me again. That isn't true. He was speaking to me, but I wasn't listening, because I was watching *Tom and Jerry* on their TV, or playing Lemmings on his Acorn computer – if that doesn't scream 'Millennial', I don't know what does.

Back at school, long after the days of swimming, we got into 'fun' group sports. Rounders was the go-to for my PE teachers when they didn't have a lesson plan. It was also one of the sports that was included in our school curriculum, and so for three months it felt like it was all we played.

I hate rounders. You walk to the home base as your entire class watches, gripping the smooth bat in your very clammy hands. Before you've had a chance to even look around, the first ball comes flying at your face.

BRAIN: Ooooh, you are definitely not going to hit this.

Unsurprisingly, I don't. It's embarrassing. A few of the boys in the class cackle at my failure. The fielders are already starting to peel off for a little break. They know that nothing is coming their way any time soon.

My PE teacher, Mrs Pennings, yells over from the side: 'Come on, Hayley, eye on the ball.'

The second ball shoots towards me.

BRAIN: Close your eyes.

No, I'm definitely not closing my eyes. Please, can we just work together here.

I've missed it again, though this time I put in quite the theatrical swing. Any chance I may have had at winning over one of the boys in my class is now well and truly out the window.

My PE teacher practically screams at me, 'Last chance, Hayley. Let's give that bat a really big swing this time.'

The bowler chucks the third ball at me. I keep my eyes on it, I swing hard and . . . the ball soars across the field, into the sky. Everyone gasps. It keeps going, and going, past birds, past planes. It's happened. I'm one of the greatest rounders players that's ever lived. Everyone runs up to me, screaming, clapping and cheering, all asking me what it's like to not only be amazing at rounders but also the coolest and cleverest girl at school.

'Hayley, get up.'

I open my eyes. I'm crouched on the floor in the foetal position, my turn over. I didn't just miss the ball, it actually smacked me square in the face. For some reason I didn't think to move. I just stood there completely lifeless as it came hurling towards me. Sadly, my nose does not bleed, so I get zero sympathy from the rest of my class and am told to head off, alone, to the side of the field. I am picked last for every single team for the next nine years.

BRAIN: I mean, sure, we were pretty bad at hitting . . . but what about throwing, let's talk about the throwing part.

I was terrible at throwing, too.

BRAIN: Yeah, this is what I like to hear, let's talk about more of your failures.

My middle school PE teacher was determined to mould me into one of the greatest throwers in my school year. I was, of course, the worst. For some reason he thought he could change this, and I assume it would have been his greatest achievement as a PE teacher to get his terrible student to master levels. This went on and on and I did not get any better. He once completely lost his temper at me for not being able to throw a discus, ball or javelin, which resulted in me crying so hard I managed to cause another nosebleed, despite the cauterisation (hello, second hot girl era, come at me boys). Thankfully, after that I was by some miracle 'medically' exempt from any other ball-touching activities.

BRAIN: That's . . . what . . . she . . .

Don't. Even. Think. About. It.

To be honest, all through my teenage years, I never managed to find a sporting activity I even enjoyed, let alone was good at. I gave athletics a shot and was pretty good at high jump, but only because I was lanky. I was able to fly swiftly through the air and land on a crash mat. It was great, and I finally felt like I was good at something.

When it got to the summer we had an athletics competition and I decided that this was my time to shine – I'd try out for high jump. I didn't make the cut. Charlie, Charlotte and Katie were all much taller and much better jumpers than I was, so I gave up the sport for good. I was, however, entered into the relay race: 100 metres with a little aluminium baton. It was basically the fun run of the day. To no one's surprise, I tripped over as the baton missed my hand and landed on my face. I tried to pick myself up, twice, but fell over my own feet. From that day on, I swore off all sports that involved anything aluminium – which I guess is the real reason I hated tap dancing.

Next, I briefly took up cross-country. I was mostly persuaded by those long-distance-running people who seem to really love it, slamming ten miles like it's a casual stroll. I still don't think that's a normal thing to be able to do. Is the human body really made for all that movement over long periods of time? I ended up stopping when I found myself spending full afternoons crouching behind hedges, only to get caught and have to do the course anyway, now partially in the dark.

In one particularly stressful period of school sports, I would pretend to faint, sometimes actually hitting my head quite hard on the way down. Aware that I was probably both stupid and committed enough to eventually self-induce a coma, Mrs Pennings began accepting any old forged note, because it was easier than dealing with my bullshit.

BRAIN: That's right. If you try hard enough, you can wear anyone down eventually. What a lesson to learn. Thanks for that.

Recently, I decided to give exercise another go. After trialling some Joe Wicks workouts in the comfort of my living room, I determined that my fitness levels were pretty good, so I signed up for the gym that's practically opposite my flat. Easy. Now I'd have no excuse to not go.

I'm a little too self-conscious to go into the actual *gym* part of the gym though – you know, with the weights and mats and . . . other stuff. Mainly because I haven't got a clue how any of it works, and also because a lot of grunting, intimidating guys hang out there, guarding the equipment. Plus, I'm pretty certain I sweat more than the average human.

> BRAIN: You definitely do. Standing near you during exercise is like taking a boat trip to Niagara Falls.

Instead, I decide to take full advantage of the classes. There are so many options. This way, at least someone will show me some moves, and there'll be a nice big crowd to blend into.

My first voluntary exercise experience is a group spin class. Riding a bike? Simple. Balls involved? Zero. What could possibly go wrong?

Turns out, a lot. Within minutes, the instructor somehow notices I am 'cheating' by not dialling up my gears enough and calls me out in front of everyone. Twice. Thanks for that. It's hard work, and I'm only 'cheating' because if I do dial the gears up like I'm being told to, I fear I might collapse and die.

When we'd started I couldn't work out how to clip my shoes onto the pedals and was too shy to ask anyone at the risk of looking like a complete newb. Now, I can't get them unclipped, leaving me stranded in a near-empty room at the end of the session, trapped on my bike pretending I'm still just cooling down. There's a nob on the front of the bike, and I'm not sure if I'm supposed to touch it.

Brain? Nob? Touch it?

BRAIN: No thanks. It's too easy.

A day later, when getting out of the shower, I notice that my entire vulva has turned a deep shade of purple. I momentarily panic that the spin bike has given me an STD. Then I realise why the older woman who was on the bike in front of me had huge, padded cycling shorts. I can't sit down for a week. I cannot put my poor vulva through that again.

Still, undeterred, and having already paid my membership for the month, I decide to try a circuit class. There are no balls, no bikes, and I've read online that you only actually exercise for 45 seconds at a time, which seems possible, even for me.

I turn up to the class to find that I am the youngest person there by 30 years. Yes, I think, this is my place, these are my people. I pick a spot and get ready for the easiest hour of my life. Some gentle stretches, mobility work, maybe even a cup of tea with the ladies at the back between sets. I start to fantasise about what it's going to feel like to be the best person in this class. For once in my entire exercise career, I'm ready to shine. The session begins. Things feel good. This is really easy.

LUNGS: I feel fantastic! This is what I was made for!

HEART: Wow, is this what it feels like to really be alive?

BRAIN: You know what, I think we should do this more often, this is so much fun!

Within minutes, everything tumbles downhill. It all started so well; I was lulled into a false sense of security. I think my lungs are going to collapse, my heart is thumping away like it's playing the drums for a heavy metal group, and instead of being quiet, my brain now literally won't shut up.

BRAIN: This is it, we're going to die! This is how we die! Get ready for the sweet release of death! We are not making it out of here alive.

I don't think I'm having a nosebleed, but I can certainly taste blood. Perhaps one of my lungs has collapsed – am I meant to tell the instructor? I feel an overwhelming urge to call out for my mum, who is hundreds of miles away from this gym. My head feels heavy and I'm sure all the blood is rushing to my big toes. This isn't right. My stomach does a flip and within seconds my head is buried deep in the little pedal bin in the corner of the room and I'm being sick. The instructor comes over with my bottle of water and tells me to breathe through the pain.

As soon as I finish throwing up, she asks if I'm ready to carry on. I'm not, but I'm too embarrassed to leave and have too much pride to say no. I wobble my way through the rest of the class, putting in just the right amount of effort to make it look like I'm still enjoying myself.

At the end of the session, a man in his late 70s gives me a little pat on the back and tells me, 'We all have to start somewhere.'

I cancel my membership on the way out and look on Rightmove for another flat to rent. I cannot be seen by any of these people ever again.

Through a period of extreme trial and error, I have finally learned that there is only one exercise for me: yoga. Lots of deep breathing, comfy mats, long stretches, a bit of meditation in a dimly lit room and . . .

BRAIN: Lying on the floor?

No, actually, it's called Shavasana. And I'm the best at it, thank you.

Brain vs The Salon

I'll never forget the first time I got highlights. In the winter, my blonde hair goes quite dark, and at 14 I was addicted to wearing it in two little pigtails. I wasn't exactly a head-turner at school, so my mousy brown hair and I basically faded into the background. The day after I went to the hairdresser and got my tresses artificially sunkissed, I strolled into school like a girl in a teen movie after she takes her glasses off. Everyone noticed me. All the guys I'd ever fancied were coming up to me and telling me my hair looked nice. It was like being a school celebrity. On that day, I learned the most important lesson of my entire school career: being popular and pretty is everything, all those movies were right all along . . .

I've been chasing that high ever since. Shiny hair, pretty nails, shoulders that sit relaxed and elegant and not all bunched up around my ears like a superhero villain – I dream of them all. But more often than not, a trip to the salon isn't the wonderland of rest and relaxation I want it to be. Sometimes, it's just horribly stressful.

Here's my assessment of the worst beauty treatments . . .

1. Going to the hairdresser

In fairy tales, looking in a mirror rarely ends well. Why, then, would we opt to sit in front of one and stare at ourselves for hours on end? Between the fluorescent lighting, frazzled roots and car mat from a Fiat Punto placed around your neck, sitting in a hairdresser's wildly spinning chair makes you feel like the 'before' in a makeover show that never ends.

I try to use my time at the hairdresser's – which can range from 40 minutes to four hours, with no rhyme or reason in what changes between those two brackets – to read a magazine or a book, but Brain usually has other ideas.

BRAIN: Oh my God, look at how many wrinkles you have! Wow, have you always been this ugly? Have you considered popping over to a plastic surgeon after this to get our face lifted? Did you realise you had one nostril bigger than the other?

After this initial roast, there's usually a short respite from Brain's brutal takedowns, as I'm escorted to a basin to have my hair washed like a little baby by another adult. Other people claim to love this part, but I genuinely don't believe them. For some reason, transferring from one salon chair to another feels wildly embarrassing. It almost always ends in me slightly losing my balance, as if I truly am a baby navigating the concept of chairs for the first time. My neck is then uncomfortably positioned over a chair sink, where I'm almost always straining my entire upper back muscles, while visibly wincing in pain.

BRAIN: Why on earth are our eyes open?!
You're staring at the ceiling like a creep.

I clamp them shut, as scalding hot water pours into my ears. The hairdresser shouts over the sloshing of the water: 'Is that temperature alright?'
I nod enthusiastically. It's not. My eyes are sealed. I will not make eye contact with a single other customer or hairdresser as we move through this humiliating ritual.
The hairdresser starts rubbing my temples. It feels quite nice actually. He's now moving his hands rhythmically across my entire scalp, like one of those spindly, gimmicky head massagers we've all owned at one point in our life. This feels, dare I say it . . . incredible.

BRAIN: What are you doing? Open your eyes, you perv. He'll think we're getting off on the head rub and, ew, why do you have a weird little smile on your face?

I open my eyes wide, assume a blank look and stare up at his forehead bobbing above me.

BRAIN: Oh God! No, close your eyes, why are you looking directly at his forehead with your mouth open?! He'll think we're in love with him.

I feel panicked, unsure whether my eyes should be open, closed or somewhere in between, like you're smizing. Perhaps that would be a little too sexy, though.

I walk back to my seat, eyes decidedly sealed shut. I'm guided by the now deeply confused hairdresser, who can't work out why he's suddenly playing a trust game with me. It feels safer for the both of us this way, though.

Back in the seat, he starts snipping away. Just an inch, I say, watching him chop off at least four. I should say it's too much, tell him that's as short as I'd like it.

BRAIN: Don't you dare question his craft. This man is a professional, and he's holding scissors! Shut the hell up and look at your phone.

For the next hour my eyes are glued to my phone as I continually open and close the same apps. There's no signal in the salon so the apps I'm sifting through are my camera roll and Apple calendar. At this point I'm worried he may have seen the close-up picture of my foot that I sent to my boyfriend to check if I had an ingrowing toe nail, and the calendar invite I have for my best friend's dog's birthday party next week.

BRAIN: He's most definitely judging you right now. You're coming across like a freak.

When the cut is done, I smile as he spins a little mirror around my head for my approval. I'm unsure what I'm supposed to be seeing, so just nod.

It looks great, so much healthier (that feels like the right thing to say).

I hand over my credit card, knowing in that moment that I will never be able to afford to buy a house. I leave the salon with a pixie cut that I didn't ask for and sit behind the wheel of my car crying into a share bag of Chilli Heatwave Doritos, looking like an escaped feral hamster.

2. Getting a wax

Waxing, to me, is a medieval torture technique designed to ruin your entire day and/or week, while removing, at best, some of your pubic hair. I only got a bikini wax for the first time last year so I could walk around on holiday without worrying that someone might notice I had hair on my body.

BRAIN: *shudder* Can you even imagine?

When you go for a wax, the first thing you have to do is pick the place that your vulva would most like to go on holiday. Does my vulva want to go to Brazil and wander naked on sandy beaches? Or is it feeling more Hollywood, with a famous strip worth visiting? In real life, my vulva mostly visits the Isle of Wight and, sadly, I think you can imagine what that looks like. The only really useful vulval hair arrangement is an arrow that points straight to the clitoris, but I don't have the confidence to pull it off, and I'm not sure even that would stop a guy from aggressively rubbing my inner thigh.

Once you're in, your beautician has you de-robe your

bottom half with the option of a pathetically small pair of paper knickers that I can't imagine anyone's bits fully fit into. It always ends up looking like you have a quivering bottom lip slipping out the side of this minuscule craft thong, so I opt to go bottom nude. She then places you into a series of unflattering yoga poses before examining your butthole and its luscious locks. While this happens, I usually try to make conversation to ease the mood.

BRAIN: OK, but talk about something normal, she has a lot of hot wax!

A selection of conversation topics I've brought up during recent waxes:

- Whether or not it is possible to understand the meaning of life in a single lifetime (her response: no).
- How childhood trauma seeps out into adult relationships (her response: please turn over).
- What I'm up to at the weekend (her response: we're done here).

The first time I had a wax, two days later I noticed the worst rash I've ever seen on my upper thigh. I immediately called 111, only for a bemused woman on the end of the line to tell me that this is a) normal, b) something I can solve with some gentle exfoliation, and c) obviously not an STD, unless I had had unprotected sex recently. I hadn't. I wish this was the dumbest reason I've called 111.

3. Receiving a massage

Having a massage is one of the most uncomfortable situations we've ever collectively pretended is fine, good, and for some reason relaxing. A stranger? Rubbing your back? Touching places you've never touched before? On a table? In a dimly lit room? No way. I'd rather have my tension, knots and backache, thank you very much.

4. Getting your nails done

Every so often I get overwhelmingly bored of my own hands and decide I should try doing something fun that feels like good self-care. Sometimes in my most deranged moments I think perhaps, with a little spit and polish, I could even be a hand model. And so, like every aspiring hand model, I go and get a manicure.

Pedicures are usually completely pointless unless you're going to sell feet pics online, which I can't be bothered to do . . . yet. Plus, the bit where they get the cheese grater out is so humiliating. I don't see anyone else having their dead foot skin being collected like Parmesan shavings. I'd rather dip myself into freezing cold water than do that again.

When you enter a nail salon, a person hands you a keyring of severed nails painted in every colour in existence, which click and clack as you try them on top of your own nails, like a serial killer wearing the face of his victims. You pretend to consider all of the colours, even though you know full well there are only three you won't regret, but in a moment of madness, you pick a wild card anyway. Neon green, how very spontaneous of me.

The woman asks me four times if I'm sure I want to go for that colour: 'It's very bright'.

I nod with conviction and tell her I'm feeling bold, then worry that I should play it safe. However, it's already too late to go back. I'd appear weak, which I am. So I hold my hands out like the tiny paws of a very good dog.

BRAIN: Why do our nails look so horrible?
It's like we've been digging a hole in the dirt
with our hands.

The nail painting begins with a ritual apology, as you explain the state of your nails to a woman who simply does not care at all. It's a choreographed dance in which you're always supposed to know where your hands should be and how they should be positioned. I for one am always getting this bit wrong and it usually results in my hands being swatted into place. Sometimes, if you're lucky, you get to sit in a massage chair, so you can jiggle around unrhythmically while they try to paint your delicate little fingers in a very precise way.

After one nail is painted neon green, she shows it to me for approval and I nod again, letting her know that, yes, I have made a good choice. She then tells me it's a very popular colour (contrary to her earlier reaction) and asks me if I'm attending a festival at the weekend. I'm not, obviously, but through sheer embarrassment I respond with a yes and then make small talk about a festival I am absolutely not attending.

Throughout this entire ordeal, you have to be very careful you don't hold her hand too tenderly, or else she'll think you love her.

I'm not sure who it was that decided we all need to do these things, or why I have somehow been reeled into it now, but here I am. I'm a sucker for freshly painted nails, regardless of the discomfort it takes me to get there.

How would I rather be spending my time? Probably getting a smear test.

Brain vs Speculum

There are so many things in life that you just assume an adult human should be able to do, but no one actually tells you how. Things like doing your taxes (I *still* have no idea), inserting a tampon, cleaning your house or plunging a toilet. I recently had to retrieve a lost tampon from my toilet pipe using a wired coat hanger and washing-up liquid. Honestly, how did people know any of this stuff before TikTok and YouTube?

> BRAIN: Remember when you found out there was a 'wrong way' to clean your house?

Yes, and now I'm suspicious of everything.

When I was two weeks away from turning 25, I received a letter in the post reminding me that it was time I booked in for my very first cervical screening. Back then, it used to be called a 'smear test', which, if I'm honest, doesn't sound like a scientific enough reason to poke something up my vagina.

BRAIN: Please, you've never needed a scientific reason before. Don't act all prudish now.

First things first, let this chapter be a little reminder to call your GP right now and book yourself into a cervical screening if you're due one. Like, now. Stop reading and do it. I'll wait.

Good. And if you're feeling nervous, settle back and enjoy the knowledge that there's nothing that can possibly happen that's worse than my first time . . .

BRAIN: Ah, the re-telling of an embarrassing story? I LOVE this bit. Let me know if you need a hand, I remember everything.

For some reason, on the day of my first vaginal inspection, I start to get really anxious about the aesthetics of my bits. Rationally, I know that medical professionals do not give a hoot about what's going on down there and if it is or isn't symmetrical. But for some reason it just felt rude not to make an effort for him or her. I'd put the effort in for a random stranger I met on a dating app two days ago, but not for a nurse? My parents would be so ashamed.

The thing is, I couldn't decide, should I be fully shaved like a little sea lion? Vajazzled like a disco queen? Or should I fashion some sort of extravagant topiary in my lady garden, perhaps a little nod to the NHS by dying my pubes blue? When it comes to pubic hair, there are so many options, but I ultimately decided to go for the classic: a full shave.

BRAIN: Very chic. It says you're bold, sassy, and you own a razor! She'll definitely think we've got our shit together.

As soon as my peach is de-fuzzed, I am on autopilot. I know I'm going to be getting my bits out, so I unthinkingly end up getting full-on ready, as if I'm about to go on a night out. I follow a YouTube tutorial on glam make-up, make my hair look a lot better than it normally does, put on clothes I feel really great in and, most importantly, make sure I've got a good pair of knickers on. I couldn't possibly wear the ones with holes in today – imagine! I look fantastic and feel like a supermodel on the walk to the doctor's office.

Everything seems fine at first. I move smoothly from the waiting room to the nurse's office and sit down for the preamble and little health questionnaire, where I'm asked about how much alcohol I drink per week (I lie, obviously).

The nurse then asks when my last period was, and I lie again, but only because I can't be bothered to do the maths and don't want to look like I'm unsure of how my own body functions. At last, it's the moment of truth. The nurse leads me behind a set of curtains and smiles warmly as she pulls them closed. 'Just pop off your bottoms and lie on the bed.'

I've got this. I've done this before, and the last time was when I had that weird sensation in my vagina which turned out to be thrush. That time, the doctor was really, really fit, and to add to the awkwardness I had a whole crew of student doctors in the room, which I could have declined, but as a people-pleaser I reluctantly obliged. All the student doctors were staring directly into my vagina as he showed them what to look for, while I worried about potentially seeing any of these people in a supermarket following my visit. Nothing could be worse than that.

This time, I'm calm, I'm confident, I'm . . . wearing a jumpsuit.

A. Fucking. Jumpsuit.

If I take my trousers off, I'm going to be fully nude. I'll be 100 per cent naked. Totally starkers. I've got my birthday suit on, and it's not even my birthday.

BRAIN: At least we're wearing a bra. It would be so embarrassing if we weren't wearing a bra.

I check. I am not wearing a bra.

Shock runs through my entire body. My eyes dart back and forth in sheer panic. This is SO much worse than the last time my vagina was swabbed. What do I do?

BRAIN: OK, stay calm. Shout 'fire!'

No, the nurse will come in, see there's no fire and realise I'm completely unhinged.

BRAIN: Run home.

But this test took months to book! Plus I'd have to run past the nurse to get to the door, and, like before, she'll realise I'm completely unhinged.

BRAIN: Fashion the jumpsuit into a top. Do Project Runway? Maybe we can just style it out! She won't even notice.

The nurse walks past the curtains, rustling them as she goes.
'Nearly ready?'
I let out a strangled: 'Not yet!'

BRAIN: Well now she's going to think we're doing something really weird in here – we've taken too long as it is.

Pure adrenaline takes over and at that moment I decide to do something that, to this day, still haunts my nightmares. I remove all of my clothes, lie down, and place a piece of the thin blue paper that they use to cover the examination table strategically over my top half. It hides nothing. The only thing I am wearing? My socks.

The nurse opens the curtain. She is stunned. She's quite obviously stifling a laugh. I am mortified. On the bright side? She can't see my real money-makers – my feet.

As she preps the test, she keeps trying to make me feel comfortable, but everything she says just makes it worse. Like, 'This happens all the time.' It definitely doesn't. And: 'I could have got you something else to wear if you'd asked.'

Too fucking late for that now. I feel like a turkey on the dining table on Christmas Day. Naked, afraid and about to be stuffed . . . sort of. She asks me to slide my butt down a bit, and I grasp onto my temporary cover-up for dear life as I shuffle my arse down. Surely there's not much more shuffling down I can do before my entire bottom half is off the table. Brain is having a field day.

> BRAIN: I bet she thinks our vulva looks weird. She's probably never seen one like that before. What if we smell? Are we meant to talk to her? Perhaps we should have taken off our socks? Did we hide our knickers?!

Obviously I've tucked my knickers into the small pocket of my jumpsuit. What a devastating thought, that this nurse could have potentially seen the very knickers that had just covered my now-naked bits.

She inserts the cold, hard speculum into my vagina and asks me what I do for a living. It's so cold, I let out a small but still audible screech. I was not prepared for any small talk, particularly while I have a duck-beak-looking dildo inside me. I try to chat in a relaxed and casual way, but can't stop thinking about the fact I'm butt-naked in a doctor's office with a woman I've just met prodding at my cervix. At least buy me a drink first, I chuckle to myself.

BRAIN: I don't mean to panic you, but I think we
need to fart.

Please, not now! Oh no, imagine if I fart in her face.
That's got to be a crime. I hold my stomach as tight as
possible, which also means I've got a better clamp on the
speculum than it probably has on me.
   She looks up: 'Try to relax.'
   No thank you, ma'am. I'm going to stay as tense as
possible. It's the only way. I wonder if it looks a bit like
I'm trying to show off my non-existent abs to her?

BRAIN: Nah, I bet she knows we're holding in a
fart, she can probably see our butthole winking at her.

The swabbing only takes about 60 seconds, but the small
talk and the prospective fart make it feel like somewhere
between five minutes and five years. As she pulls out the
speculum, I cringe, wondering if it has come out covered
in my discharge.

BRAIN: I don't mean to be helpful, but that really
is the least of your problems right now.

At last, we're done. The nurse tells me I did a very good
job, which makes me feel oddly proud of myself, though
I've accomplished absolutely nothing, as she was the one
doing all the work. Just as it usually is when I'm naked on
a stranger's bed, actually.

The nurse pulls the curtain back around me, which feels like a pointless exercise. Isn't it supposed to help me maintain my dignity? I'm already fully naked. Her seeing me put my clothes back on is hardly going to be embarrassing now, is it?

On the other side of the curtain, I hear her say, 'Just head to reception whenever you're ready.'

The door to the room swings closed and I finally relax. I did it. It's over. Thank goodness. And I let out the biggest, loudest, most rip-roaring fart of my entire life. The examination table shakes like it's in an earthquake.

I pull on my jumpsuit, sweep back the curtain, and there she is.

'Just came back in for my notes.'

BRAIN: Are you sure you don't want to run?

So what's the moral of this story? Book your smear test. Never wear a jumpsuit. Don't worry about your pubes. And probably don't fart until you're 100 per cent certain you're alone, unless you're far more fart confident than I am. Also, thank your nurses, they work harder than any of us can ever imagine; just don't say 'well done' patronisingly to them after your cervix has been prodded.

How to Cover Up a Fart

Farting is a universal fact of human existence. We all do them, and if you don't, there might be something wrong with you – maybe go and see a doctor. Farting is normal, so it's incredibly odd that we've collectively decided that it is the most embarrassing thing that can ever happen to a human being. And there's nothing more mortifying than farting in front of a new partner. We all know that when you're vetting someone you might want to spend some – or even all – of your life with, the most important thing is to never, ever let them know that you fart. I'm no psychologist or sociologist or whoever's job it is to know about fart culture, but I can tell you one thing: humans are irrational, and I want no part of it. Set those farts free.

Holding in a fart is no good. You end up with stomach pains, and eventually – because you've been holding it in for so long – you end up internally farting and, frankly, I think that's an even worse thing for your lover to hear. Your butt grumbling like an angry bear? Terrifying.

I can understand that you may not feel comfortable letting loose straight away. To ease yourself in gently, I advise that during the early stages of a relationship it's important that you and your new love interest only hang out at old houses and/or duck ponds. That way, if you accidentally let a ripping great fart slip out, you can blame a creaky floorboard or a guilty-looking duck.

I can't afford a creaky old house, but thankfully I am now a pro at stealth farting, so I've compiled a list of techniques for how to cover up a fart, whether you're in bed with a lover or just navigating a trip around a supermarket after a three-bean taco (this is what I call my lover).

The Distractor

You're in the danger zone; a huge fart is brewing and there's nothing you can do to stop it. My advice is to cough hard and loud for a long time. Coughing is one of the most distracting noises a human can make, other than perhaps a scream, but I can't in good conscience advise you to scream just to cover a parp. Can you imagine? Everyone walking around screaming all the time? Talk about the outside world reflecting my inner life.

A cough also sounds a little bit like a fart, so if you

time it exactly right and put enough welly into your performance, you can generate an indistinguishable cacophony of noise – a fantasia, if you will. Just keep an ear on the sound levels or you might find that your trumpet is louder than your bark.

The Butt Muffler

This is my favourite type of cover-up, but it only works when you're already in the bathroom. It's perfect for those times when a carpet frog is trying to pull a Harry Houdini while you're mid-stream. After all, there's nothing less forgiving than a bottom burp echoing around a porcelain poop chamber, particularly when your lover is in earshot.

The trick? Grab a wad of toilet roll, layer it up and place it (gently) against your butthole. This is a sure-fire way to silence the air biscuit, so you can get back to pretending you have no bodily functions at all.

Spread 'Em

This one is simple but effective – an 'it does what it says on the tin' kind of thing. Pull those cheeks apart and let that silent bottom burp whisper out of your butt like a warm breeze in August. Honestly, I'm not super confident on this one, but I've heard other people swear it works. Maybe test it out a couple of times first. Oh, and make sure you only try it when the tank is empty, if you know what I mean.

The Squeeze

In many ways the spiritual opposite of the Spread 'Em, this one is all about focus. Right as Trump is about to exit the White House, clench everything really tight and get ready for a controlled release. Like an air mattress that is slowly deflating, your intestinal vapours will slowly and silently dissipate. The important thing here is to avoid anything that could give you a fright, as any sudden movements will undo all your good work and give everyone around you the scare of their life.

The Kicker

If you're in bed with a hottie and you've managed to produce a silent but deadly backdoor breeze, first of all, well done you. There's still a chance they'll never find out what you've done. The key here is to pull the covers tight around you to create a personal hotbox for the stench – in a sexy way, if you can – before kicking a tiny air hole out of the bottom of the duvet with your foot. Warning: this can backfire on a hot day if there's a fan near the end of the bed.

Loud and Proud

If you really want to make an impression on someone, or find out if they truly are 'The One', just let it
rip as loud and as abruptly as possible without saying a
word. It's going to happen eventually, so you might as
well embrace it. Plus, they've definitely been farting this
whole time too. Gross . . .

Vagina's Lullaby

I once read in a guide to lucid dreaming that before you go to sleep you can pre-program your dreams. In all honesty, I skimmed most of the book, but from what I gathered it's pretty easy. All you need to do is think of the people, places and scenarios you want to dream about and, as if by magic, you land exactly where you want to when you drift off. Simple. Obviously I started by trying to pre-program some sex dreams.

Scenario 1: The Superyacht

As I lay my head on the pillow, I close my eyes and picture myself dressed in a beautiful white playsuit.

BRAIN: Hang on a second. A white playsuit? Do we work on the ship?

No, I'm a guest. Scratch that, actually, I own the ship.

Yeah, in this fantasy I'm not just milling around on fancy yachts, I'm also super rich. So I can pretty much wear whatever I like.

> BRAIN: But what if we get our period? There's not a stain-remover on earth that can scrub blood out of white cotton.

I won't get my period! It's a dream. Obviously I'm in control of what happens.

> BRAIN: No, I reckon ditch the playsuit. I think we should go for something that floats. I'm not sure we're that strong at swimming – remember when we almost drowned in that shark reef because you saw a baby shark?

Thanks for bringing that up. That had nothing to do with my swimming abilities.

> BRAIN: Maybe wear a wetsuit, to be safe?

I'm not wearing a wetsuit in my sex dream.

> BRAIN: Well, I'm just saying, we should probably be a bit more practical.

I'm dressed in a pair of practical black shorts, a white t-shirt and black platformed sandals, wandering along the sun-drenched marina in Capri. I spot a tall, handsome man with piercing blue eyes, and arms so big he could carry over ten shopping bags containing tins of baked beans and liquids without so much as breaking a sweat. Wow, imagine what he could do to little old dainty me.

He strides towards me, announcing that he must take me onto his yacht immediately so we can have sex. He lifts me with just one of his giant hands and holds me high in his palm like I'm a tiny mouse, so cute and nimble. He points towards the biggest superyacht I've ever seen. His legs are enormous, so we're there within three strides. Crowds are forming around us, whooping and cheering as we climb aboard his yacht, 'The Incredible Hunk'. He lays my tiny body onto the round, spinning bed (very retro) in his cabin and tears off his string vest, revealing his huge, bulging . . .

I slowly slip into a deep slumber. This is it.

Suddenly the sky turns, it's the middle of the night and the waves are beating against the side of the boat. The hunky man goes to the window, where he is pulled by a giant tentacle down into the thrashing waves. 'No, wait! I thought we were going to have sex!' I scream into the storm. But my screams are muted, suffocated. I can't make any sound. I try once more . . .

I wake up, panting breathlessly, and check my phone. The time is 3.08am – the witching hour. I tap my sweaty brow with the back of my hand and close my eyes, hoping to be taken to an improved, happier version of this dream.

Damn it. I'm back on the yacht, bobbing helplessly at sea. I stare out at the horizon. Another massive tentacle rises from the water and grabs me around my waist, pulling me under. It's a giant sea monster, Pablo – part whale, part fish, part octopus, part beefcake? Wow, this is unexpected. Under the waves, we lock eyes and . . . I immediately feel a connection. What? Is THIS what I want? Is it technically bestiality? Do I even care? I lean forward to kiss my scaly prince, Pablo. He leans in too. Here's where the dream really picks up, I think. My head is ripped from my body. I am dead.

I wake up. I've got my period.

BRAIN: Told you we should have worn a wetsuit.

It takes me weeks to get over my sex dream with the sea beefcake, Pablo. I'm too scared to have a bath, for fear of what it will ignite in me. He said more in that one look than any man has ever said to me in my whole life. I swipe left on anyone who says they like going to the beach or watersports in their dating profile. I can't even flush the toilet without having flashbacks.

Scenario 2: The Cabins

A couple of months later, once I've stopped breaking out in a cold sweat at the sound of a running tap, I decide to try again. I slip into my duvet wearing the sexiest pyjamas

I own and turn off the lights. In this scenario, I've come to the countryside to escape real life. I want a break. No, I need a break. I feel burnt out and need some time away from all the screens I have to look at every day.

BRAIN: Come on, this is way too close to real life. A fantasy should be fun. What about that sea monster beefcake thing?

No! No more sea beefcakes. In fact, this bit of countryside couldn't be further from the sea, or from anywhere. It's completely remote. Miles from civilisation. I am free.

I brush my hair behind my left ear, take a quick selfie surrounded by all this nature, and upload it to my Instagram story.

BRAIN: So there's 5G in the forest? Better check those emails, we might have something from our manager.

There's no 5G so my story fails to upload. I turn my phone to flight mode, dig a hole in the soil and bury it.

BRAIN: Digging? Great. Very sexy. Good luck explaining this to your manicurist.

I grab my beige, overpriced Urban Outfitters tote bag and slip it over my shoulder, reminding me how much I care about the planet. I walk slowly towards my log cabin as I gaze up at the tall trees.

Suddenly, a man with kind eyes and big meaty legs stops me in my tracks. He's so big, and visibly tough. It looks like he could single-handedly work the door at Slug and Lettuce in Leicester Square on a bank holiday weekend. He's got an axe in one hand. Is he . . . a lumberjack?

BRAIN: So another big guy? Sounds like someone has daddy issues.

He's nothing like my dad, don't spin this. He does, however, tell me to follow him, and leads me towards this huge bird aviary he's built. Momentarily, I think about pulling out my phone to snap a quick picture for Instagram, but I remember I've buried my phone in the soil, and anyway there's still no 5G. His hand brushes mine and my breath catches in my throat as he exhales sharply. In this moment, I know we're going to have hot, passionate sex.

We stand there looking up at all the tropical birds. 'Oh look, it's a parakeet!' I exclaim to this unnamed but beautiful man. He corrects me and tells me it's a wood pigeon before gently patting me on the head and laying me down on his makeshift bed, full of straw and stuff.

I fall sound asleep.

The birds' eyes are suddenly black as night, and they're nose diving towards us as I try desperately to bat them off with the pillows from the makeshift bed. I look down, and the pillows are made of bags of ham, only baiting these feral flying creatures further. Immediately, the pigeons tear my woodland hunk limb from limb. He looks like a bag of crushed shrimp tails. Our love? An impossible jigsaw.

I panic and try to run to the door of the aviary only to find it's stuck. I try with all my strength to break the door down. But it's too late, the birds descend on me in a flurry of wings and shrimpy pieces of my lumberjack love. Our love? An impossible jigsaw.

I wake with a jump to find I'm in my own bed. Not a bird in sight. Thank God. This time, I reach over to my bedside table, grab my Womaniser clit stimulator (if God made vibrators), and take matters into my own hand.

Eventually, I fall back into a deep, satisfied sleep.

Abruptly, I find that I am in my old primary school. My boyfriend is there, but he looks like my cousin's puggle, Roo. There's a sudden urge inside me. I need to pee, so I walk down the school hallway to the toilets. I open the door, but every surface is covered with bugs. Sexy bugs, sure, but bugs nonetheless.

I run to the next door, to find every teacher I've ever had washing each other's hair. It's super sexy, but I don't know why. I realise peeing here would just be disrespectful. Behind the next door, it's the sea beefcake, Pablo. A pang in my heart. He's chopping wood with his giant tentacles and it's hot as hell.

The next door? Some of the fittest wood pigeons I have ever seen. Everyone and everything is trying to have sex with me, in one huge subconscious orgy.

Standing in the hallway, I pull down my feathery knickers and release an almighty stream of piss.

I wake up. I have wet the bed.

BRAIN: Like I said, we should have worn a—

Shut up.

Brain vs Health Anxiety

The first time I had a panic attack, it was nothing like I'd seen in films or on TV. I'd always assumed a panic attack involved two key elements:

1. Realising you're having a panic attack, because it's incredibly obvious with all the hyperventilating.
2. Breathing into a paper bag until you're fine again.

Oh, how wrong I was.

My first brush with death is in my first year of university. I'm laying on an ancient, dusty sofa watching *The Great British Bake Off*. Last night was a bit of a wild one, so I'm morbidly hungover, as every student usually is. At this point in my tried-and-tested recovery process, I'm more Lucozade Sport than woman. My housemate Scarlett is collapsed on the other sofa, also hungover, but doesn't look it one bit. She's unenthusiastically commenting on

Urvashi's Japanese lime cupcakes, though she's munching on a bowl of dry cereal which I feel may revoke her ability to judge any of these bakers.

Here, plopped between questionable throw cushions, my chest starts to feel really, really tight. It's like someone has tied a rubber band around my lungs.

DOCTOR BRAIN: I see you're having
problems breathing.

Recently, Brain has become convinced that she knows if not *everything*, then at least *something* about medicine. This is because I've been watching loads of *Casualty*, and I'm not prepared to stop, so I have to indulge her. Plus, she might be right – she's even started referring to herself as Doctor Brain during medical emergencies.

DOCTOR BRAIN: I just checked your pulse,
it's beating completely out of rhythm.

I put my fingers to my neck and try to feel for a beat. Nothing. I can't feel anything at all. Oh my God, am I dead?

I move my hand a bit more and there it is: my pulse. OK, not dead, but it does feel a bit . . . uneven? And fast. Like it's playing the drum part of 'Seven Nation Army' in a really rubbish cover band.

DOCTOR BRAIN: Hayley, this is serious.
You're having a heart attack.

A heart attack? But I'm so young! There's so much I haven't done. I don't think I'm under enough stress for this to be happening. I realise I've never visited Japan, or tried any of the weird Coke flavours, like Cherry or Lime. Slowly, without wanting to draw too much attention to myself, I reach for my phone and open WebMD.

DOCTOR BRAIN: This is a good idea.

I search my symptoms: tight chest, shortness of breath, dizzy, thirsty. That last one could be the hangover, but how would I know?

The website asks: do you have shooting pains in your left arm?

DOCTOR BRAIN: Choose 'yes'.

Do I? I don't think I can feel any shooting pains in either of my arms.

DOCTOR BRAIN: You might not be able to feel them, but that doesn't mean they're not happening. Obviously you're having a heart attack so you're probably distracted.

I click yes. The results pop up.

DOCTOR BRAIN: Exactly as I thought. You're having a heart attack.

Suddenly the room starts spinning. Everything looks strange. My eyes feel like they have a mind of their own and it seems as though everything around me is getting closer and closer. I'm overwhelmingly tired. Maybe if I just close my eyes for a second . . .

DOCTOR BRAIN: STAY WITH ME, HAYLEY. DON'T LOOK INTO THE LIGHT. BY WHICH I MEAN, LOOK INTO THE LIGHT.

I hold my eyes open and stare directly into the overly white ceiling light. Everything is blurry and warped. I should probably tell Scarlett what's happening.

DOCTOR BRAIN: No way! We've only known her three months. Can you actually imagine how embarrassing it'll be. God, it's not worth thinking about. Don't you dare say a word. Better to just die in silence.

I let out a small, barely audible, guttural moan, and Scarlett turns towards me anyway.

'Hayley, are you OK? You don't look right.'

Cover blown. I have no other choice but to confess: I'm dying.

This is serious news. She pauses *Bake Off*.

Luckily, Scarlett owns a car, so she and the boys we live with bundle in and head straight to A&E, via Pizza

GoGo (they have extra-large pizzas for £5; it's the only way to keep everyone's energy up during the hangover from hell). I'm still finding it hard to breathe, but I do feel better knowing that my chances of dying on a sofa where possibly thousands of students have shagged has just dropped significantly.

Hang on. How many students HAVE shagged on that sofa? Could I be . . . pregnant? From watching *Bake Off* on a jizz-encrusted couch? Maybe I'm about to give birth to a little sofa baby. With the array of different ejaculations sampled on those cushions, I wonder if it'll be some sort of superhuman baby with dozens of fathers.

DOCTOR BRAIN: We can't rule anything out.

My mind is racing. At the doors of the hospital, I'm put in a wheelchair and pushed into the waiting room. It all feels a bit dramatic but at the same time completely necessary. The usual suspects are all there: a small child with a huge bruise, a man with his hand wrapped in a bloody tea towel, a woman who is coughing everywhere without covering her mouth. Everyone is trying to look as sick as possible, so they can be seen first. I know their game.

DOCTOR BRAIN: Why are you not passing out on the floor? Screaming out in pain?

Don't be silly. I'm not going into labour (at least, I hope not).

DOCTOR BRAIN: But you are having a heart attack! Do you want to die here?!

I really, really don't. Dying in the comfort of my own home is scary enough, but dying here in this hospital with its sterile walls and sickly detergent smell? I don't know the afterlife rules, but I fear my ghost could be trapped here forever. I realise I need to play the game.

It turns out, when I'm really scared I might die, I can suddenly pull an Oscar-worthy performance out of the bag. I begin by quietly wailing, throwing myself around a bit in the wheelchair. It attracts a couple of the receptionists' eyes. I'm definitely making some progress on the invisible list of who gets to be seen first.

I dial it up a little more. I can't tell if I'm doing it for attention now, or if I'm genuinely freaking out, to the point where I feel completely out of control. I'm not even embarrassed, which is odd because I'm always embarrassed. Embarrassment is my default state. I can't even cross the road without feeling as though every single person is looking at me. It's like being centre stage. The drivers are bored waiting for the lights to change and have nowhere else to look but at the pavement where you're stood. It feels as though you've forgotten how to move properly, and you walk across the road with dead straight legs and arms flopping about at your sides. It's a horrifying experience and I'll often walk miles out of my way just to avoid crossing a road.

I leap out of the chair and cling to the receptionist's desk.

'Help me, I can't breathe!'

A nurse pokes her head out from a side room and ushers me in. She tells me to lie down on a bed and instructs me to take long, deep breaths and to focus on a point in front of me while she asks me a series of questions:

1. Do you smoke?
2. Have you been drinking?
3. Have you taken any substances?
4. What medication do you take, if any?
5. Do you have any pain or discomfort in your arms or legs?
6. Has this happened before?
7. Could you be pregnant?

I don't hear any of them because Doctor Brain is yelling.

DOCTOR BRAIN: TELL HER ABOUT THE SUPERHUMAN SOFA BABY.

I'm definitely not going to tell a real clinician about the jizz-encrusted sofa. I can't actually be pregnant; I haven't had sex for months.

I catch my reflection in a small mirror above the sink and am shocked to see a ghost staring back at me. My skin is white, almost grey, and there are huge rings around my eyes. The image of me haunting this hospital forever returns. This simply cannot happen, I cannot die here. I turn back to find the nurse prepping a huge needle. She's going to do a blood test.

DOCTOR BRAIN: Hang on . . . needles? No way. In my medical opinion, we're completely recovered. We should go home immediately. Come on, get up. We're leaving, NOW.

I try to stand up, but I can't. I'm shaking. Before I can explain, the nurse takes my arm and lurches for the vein.

I see stars. Everything goes dark. I've passed out.

I wake up, and retch into a bean-shaped cardboard bowl thrust underneath my chin. Turns out my fear of needles is still very much a problem. The nurse leaves to process the results.

DOCTOR BRAIN: What will you call the sofa baby? I think Armchair for a boy or Chaise Longue for a girl.

Eventually, a doctor enters the room. He is holding a clipboard and wearing a pair of very academic-looking glasses. The look on his face tells me he's about to say something extremely serious. I brace myself.

'We've run your blood, and you'll be pleased to know everything looks really normal.'

DOCTOR BRAIN: No, that can't be right. I'm a professional! I've got a degree from Google! I'm far more educated than he is.

I blink at him. He tries again, 'Have you ever had a panic attack before?'

Hang on a second. A panic attack? I had a panic attack? With no rapid breathing or brown paper bags? How could this be? I am beyond mortified and feel like a complete fool. I can't believe I wasted everyone's time on something that definitely didn't need medical attention. I think of all those people in the waiting room and experience a surge of guilt. I try to recall every person in there. I don't think anyone looked too critical, which eases my guilt slightly.

I head home, too embarrassed to answer my house-mate's questions, then sulk off to my room. They watch the rest of *Bake Off* without me.

My next brush with death happens in the middle of October, months after my humiliating hospital visit. All my housemates have gone home for half term, but I've stayed behind so I can catch up on some coursework before heading back to the Isle of Wight to see my family. I'm working on my laptop in bed when I feel a weird sensation in my head and my eyes begin to blur.

DOCTOR BRAIN: It's a brain tumour.

Don't panic, it's fine, and definitely not a brain tumour. I'll just take some ibuprofen and it'll probably go away.

DOCTOR BRAIN: Ibuprofen?! Absolutely not. What if it makes it worse? You're far too lazy to read all the side-effects and I am certain if we take any, we will die.

Are you joking? It's literally sold in supermarkets. I take it all the time. Even children can have it.

Still, my chest feels quite tight and there's a warm pain rising in my stomach.

DOCTOR BRAIN: Wait right there, I'm Googling.

No, don't do that!

DOCTOR BRAIN: Just as I suspected. This is terminal. We may only have a matter of hours, maybe minutes left.

What should I do?

DOCTOR BRAIN: In my medical opinion, it's time to panic!

Brain tells me to call an ambulance. I recall my trip to A&E and decide against it. Instead, I manage to phone my dad. In hysterics, I tell him I'm dying. In his most calm, reassuring voice, he tells me to sit on my bed, take deep breaths and focus on something in front of me, just like the nurse did last time. Somehow this works and I don't die. It's like some sort of miracle, like maybe I've just narrowly escaped death this time.

When I arrive home a few days later, Dad persuades me to book in with my GP. I tell her my symptoms, along with everything else I've been thinking and feeling over the last few years, including my two scrapes with death, and the other 10+ times I've felt like I might die but didn't.

All the horror stories of sick people I've known circle around my head. There was a girl at a school near where I lived who had been sick for a year. She kept fainting and having nosebleeds. Everyone dismissed her symptoms and told her she was fine, but it turned out she had cancer. She survived, thankfully, but the story sticks with me.

There was also a girl at my school, the year below me, and her parents were getting divorced so she was really stressed. Her periods stopped, she was vomiting all the time and the doctor signed her off school with stress. A month later she gave birth in her bathroom.

Talking to the doctor fills me with a sense of impending doom. I am sure I am going to be told something terrible is happening.

DOCTOR BRAIN: Like I said, this is definitely a brain tumour.

The doctor asks me if I've ever experienced anxiety before.

'No, I'm not anxious,' I reply.

But . . . am I?

'Do you often feel dizzy, or restless?'

I think of all the times in the day when my stomach churns for seemingly no reason at all, or when I get short of breath thinking about doing new things. Or when I feel so nauseous I can't eat.

'How about sleep, do you sleep well?'

Not really. I lie awake most nights thinking about what made the stains on the ceiling, or how I'm going to die, or if the stain on the ceiling is because someone died upstairs and no one noticed so now their body juice is just leaking through the carpet above me. Maybe one day the ceiling will get so weak from the juice it'll cave in and everything will fall on me and I'll suffocate.

'Have you ever had a panic attack?'

Well, it wasn't like the ones they have in the movies, but yeah, after the comment in A&E, I guess I've had one or two.

'Hayley, I think you have something called generalised anxiety disorder.'

DOCTOR BRAIN: Just as I suspected, I knew this all along.

What? No, you didn't! You told me I was dying.

DOCTOR BRAIN: Now, now. Just take deep breaths and focus on a point in front of us.

The doctor carefully explains what anxiety is, before listing some strategies I can use, like exercising more and drinking less. She tells me that my anxiety might make me want to stay inside more, that it can make me feel panicked in social situations and that I may have difficulty concentrating. I listen carefully. I can't believe there's a name for so many of the things I've been going through. It feels like this, at last, is a chance to take control of my life.

Finally, she says, 'I think you should try therapy.'

DOCTOR BRAIN: But that would mean we have to talk to a stranger. We couldn't possibly do that.

Definitely True Facts about Brain

1. The human brain contains about one hundred million neurones and two hundred million memories of all the minor embarrassing things you've done that absolutely no one else noticed.
2. The brain isn't fully formed until around 25 years, so you legally can't be held responsible for anything you did as a teenager (I'm not a lawyer, so don't quote me on this).
3. 75 per cent of the brain is made up of water, so, in a way, your thoughts are both literally and figuratively swimming around in your head.
4. Our brains get smaller as we age until they're roughly the size of a golf ball, which is why old people are so obsessed with it. It's all so clear now.
5. Information in your brain travels at around 268 mph, which is faster than a Formula One car, but still slower than your colleague telling

you every detail about their new spreadsheet that you absolutely did not ask about.

6. The average brain generates 48.6 thoughts per minute, and only 48 of them are about your weird crush on Nigel from the local corner shop.

7. Albert Einstein's brain was slightly smaller than average, which proves that size really doesn't matter.

8. It's a myth that you only use 10 per cent of your brain. You actually use all of it – you're just not as good at maths as that girl you went to school with, and humans will never be capable of telepathy.

9. There is no evidence that the human attention span is getting shorter, except for . . . hang on, what was I talking about?

Brain vs Poop

It is a truth universally acknowledged that children cannot wipe their own arses. What you don't realise at the time is that, rather than being humiliating, these are actually the glory days. That's right, I've said it: I don't love wiping my own arse. Or anyone else's, for that matter. Sue me. It's a boring, sometimes laborious task and frankly I've long felt that the countries with bidets have got it right: we should all be washing our arses after we poop; it just makes sense.

My parents never shamed me for not being able to do it, but unfortunately this meant that for a long time I had no incentive to learn. In my kid's brain, I just assumed their lack of urgency meant that it was a mutually beneficial situation – fun for them and a luxury for me – that I should drag out for as long as possible. I'm descended from a long and powerful line of IBS sufferers, so I also assumed that chatting about poo in a casual and relaxed way was a normal state of affairs. Poo! We all do it! And we talk about it all the time, right?

BRAIN: No one else talks about poo as much as you.

Everyone has famous stories about their childhood that their parents love to dredge up on important occasions like birthdays, weddings and funerals. Probably not the same one for all three, but you never know. For me, these stories are all poo-related. For instance, on my wedding day, my mum will probably stand up to say, 'When Hayley was two years old, I was busy on a work call when she loudly announced she needed to poo. Because I was busy, she took herself, but after completing the deed, she immediately realised she didn't know how to wipe . . .'

BRAIN: Pause for applause. Pause for laughter. Pause for second round of applause.

'. . . so she came back out with her pants around her ankles and announced "Mum, can you come and wipe my bum?" to an entire conference call of old men. I told her I'd be a couple of minutes, but instead of waiting, she headed back to the toilet. There, she proceeded to unspool an entire roll of toilet paper – and I mean an entire roll – and stuff it into the bowl.'

BRAIN: Everyone at the wedding is crying with joy. This is a story that will go down in history. Your husband is standing on the table, miming shoving wads of toilet paper into a pipe. You've never felt more in love.

'Then, she decided to flush the toilet, flooding the entire house. I only noticed because there was water dripping through the ceiling, at which point I rushed upstairs to find her sobbing violently while paddling around in a puddle of shit and soggy toilet paper.'

BRAIN: Your husband gets down on one knee and proposes to you once again. He is obsessed.

Still, that story is nothing compared to the one they'll tell at my funeral. Make sure you get an invite, you won't want to miss it.

The Great Flood of '95 should have encouraged me to put the time in to learning to wipe my arse properly, but instead it did the opposite. I came away from the experience thinking that not only should I never poo again but that, if I must, I simply *had* to be accompanied by a responsible adult. There was no way I was reliving the trauma of almost drowning in my own faeces.

Three years later, I started primary school. I had my book bag (to this day the most exciting bag I've ever owned – Balenciaga, take notes), my tiny school uniform, and my hair tied tight in two high ponytails on either side of my head. I was officially a big girl. This was it, I was raring to go.

Day one, I settled into my new classroom. Sitting

between my pint-sized new friends, I had just begun the serious academic task of arranging pasta into shapes with Pritt Stick when I felt my tummy rumble. I raised my hand and asked to go to the toilet, expecting to be accompanied by my teacher, Mrs Neiddu. However, instead of holding my hand and coaching me through it as I had come to expect from any nearby grown-up, she simply waved me off towards the toilet door. I was left to my own devices. Straight away, the familiar concerns arose. How much paper do you use? Which direction do you wipe? When do you stop? I couldn't risk flooding the school, so at the top of my lungs I shouted, 'Mrs Neiddu, Mrs Neiddu!'

She never came, so I never wiped. I simply hopped off the bowl, pulled up my pants and tights and headed back to class. I got away with it, or so I thought, until I went to my cousin's wedding a mere 20 years later, only to find that Mrs Neiddu's daughter was the maid of honour. As I introduced myself, she leant in and said:

'Oh yeah, I remember my mum telling me about how you refused to wipe your arse.'

BRAIN: Well, it's not the best story, but at least someone's talking about your poop at a real wedding! Dreams really do come true!

As an adult, I'm obviously more than competent at wiping my own arse. I'm actually really good at it now. In fact, when it comes to poop in general, I feel relatively on top of things in the butt department. Or at least I did, until I went on holiday with my first boyfriend.

Like all great romances, Jake and I met on a night out at uni. I was shit-faced, drinking a bottle of VK, dressed as a giant baby, complete with nappy and dummy, while he was dressed like Russell Brand. I later learned he was not actually dressed like Russell Brand, he just looked a bit like Russell Brand and they shared a similar sense of style. I don't know who thought it was a good idea to go on a night out dressed as a giant baby, but it seemed to do the trick. Perhaps this should have been my first red flag with Jake.

Jake and I shared a number of hobbies, including going out, sleeping in and drinking coffee, but the one thing we both really wanted to do was go on holiday together. At that time in my life, I couldn't imagine anything more glamorous than going abroad with a lover. Even if the lover in question was a boy in his early 20s who still used his mother's credit card to buy things, and once got genuinely annoyed that I forgot to tag him in an Instagram post.

Ten months into this whirlwind romance, we finally did it. The plan was to head to Turkey, where we would spend two weeks together, then Jake would head home before my family joined me for a final week. Three whole weeks abroad. I was feeling incredibly smug and excited, right up until the day before we were due to leave, when in a completely unrelated conversation, Jake suddenly said, 'Girls don't poop.'

Look, I know this sounds nuts, but I wanted to impress

this guy so much. He had always reminded me how out of my league he was. He'd tell me I was 'punching' and that, 'A lot of girls are interested in me,' so I just nodded along, desperate for his approval. Who was I to break the news to the guy that women have bowels, and functioning ones at that? I wanted him to look at me and see a sexy, gorgeous woman, not a walking, talking poop machine, which all my family knew I was. Don't all women want this? Look at my boobs! Forget about the poop!

BRAIN: Sometimes I think sexism isn't the problem, it's you.

But you'd been together for ten months, I hear you scream. Yes, and in that time I'd been arranging my schedule entirely around poop-portunities that were as far away from him as possible. And so far I had managed to get away with it. I pride myself in my ability to poop fast, so suspicions had never arisen. I mean, really, I'd brought this on myself.

I started to really stress out about this trip. Imagine if he looked at my butt while I was wearing a bikini and instead of thinking, 'How did I end up with a girl that has an arse flatter than her chest?' He'd think, 'Gross, that's where she shits from.'

It couldn't be me.

BRAIN: Don't panic! I'm on it. After all, I'm the one in charge of everything here.

By day ten of the holiday, I'm still yet to take a shit. It's not intentional. There are plenty of opportunities outside of our hotel room where I could do it and still keep up the ruse, but for some reason my bowels aren't playing ball. By now, my stomach is in serious pain and it's hard as a rock. Not to toot my own horn, but I usually poop like clockwork twice a day. Every morning, we wake up and head straight to the pool, where my stomach pushes up against my swimsuit and I have to clasp a towel like a baby in front of it. I can't believe I'm so young and already a mother of one (towel) with another (poop) on the way. On the morning of day ten, I call my dad in hushed whispers from the hotel corridor, where he tells me to try adding a spoonful of olive oil to my drinks to get things moving. If Jake thought my breakfast of six oily coffees was unusual, he chose not to say anything. I guess he thinks that, unlike shitting, this is 'just a girl thing'.

Day eleven and I've told Jake I'm heading to the shops to buy some more sunscreen, despite the fact that we obviously have loads. There, I fill a basket with prunes, apricots and an artichoke, which I have no way of cooking but have heard works, so am going to try eating it raw. I smuggle my haul back to the room and chow down while Jake is in the shower. I'm full of dried, fibrous foods – surely this will get things moving? At dinner, while Jake eats his normal food, I head to the restaurant toilet and crouch on the floor, willing my stomach to do something, anything. But alas, no luck.

This sparks a memory from when I was younger,

when just walking into a bathroom store would conjure up something in my bowels. It'd be a mad rush for my parents to pick out new bathroom fittings before I begged to take a shit in a disconnected toilet. Eventually they had to start tag-teaming. My dad would wait in the car with me while my mum went in and drew a map of all the toilets, sinks and tiles she liked the look of. He'd then go in and use the map to find her picks. They'd dart in and out with me in the car, making their final decisions. It was the only way they could do these trips without me causing chaos in the showroom. I google bathroom stores nearby, but apparently there aren't any in the tourist area of Bodrum.

Day twelve and now I'm really panicking. I am struggling to eat anything. I head straight to a pharmacy (under the pretence of needing even more sunscreen) to buy some laxatives. At least, I think they're laxatives. I mime taking a shit to the pharmacist, which involves a lot of squatting, belly rubbing and painful strained faces, so they're either laxatives, birth control pills or some kind of sedative. I take them and wait. Nothing. Perhaps it was the latter.

Day thirteen and I am more poop than woman now. I start googling 'poop surgically removed from body' and think about how it will probably be cheaper to get it done while I'm still in Turkey, rather than waiting until I'm back in the UK. I start to wonder if anyone has ever died from not being able to shit.

BRAIN: What a way to go, very *you*.

The heat is making me feel incredibly nauseous. At dinner, the waiter gives me a dirty look as he hands me a sugary cocktail. He thinks I'm pregnant and having twins. Jake leaves in the morning, so this is meant to be a nice final night, but I can barely concentrate. About an hour into my kid's menu meal (it's literally all I can stomach), Jake asks me why I'm just pretending to eat my dinosaur nuggets and I finally break. 'I haven't pooped for two whole weeks because you don't think girls shit. Now my body believes it and I look like I'm about to give birth at any minute.'

He stares at me in shock. He doesn't say a word, just laughs hysterically. At least I think he's laughing, but I can barely hear him, because my ears are blocked with poop. I sit and wonder how many shits he's taken with ease while we've been away, and my love turns to hatred.

The next day, we say goodbye, and I head over to my parents' hotel. As I step over the threshold of their room, I can practically hear my bowels kicking into action. I dodge and duck their welcome hugs and run towards their bathroom.

BRAIN: Stand back, she's gonna blow!

Most people aren't brave enough to write in their book about the most magnificent shit of their life, but I'm not most people. I'll think about that dump until the day I die. Three weeks of bowel movements flowed out of me like a human sewage pipe, and I loved every second of it.

Forty-five minutes later I rise from the toilet like a queen from her throne. I'm a new woman! I'm lighter than air! I've never felt happier! Freed from the shackles of 30 pounds of faecal matter, my future is brighter than it's ever been. I float from the bathroom and apologise to my parents. They don't care. They can see the joy on my face and it's all they've ever dreamed of for their daughter.

As soon as the plane lands back in the UK, I call Jake to break up with him. There are lots of things I want in my life – love, success, a cute little rescue dog – but more than anything, I want to be able to take a shit.

How to Get Over a Break-Up

Break-ups are the worst. One minute you're lounging in bed with your beloved on a Sunday morning, finishing each other's Wordles. The next, you're Instagram-stalking their new partner over a huge glass of wine, wondering if all your friends think they're hotter than you. You pick them apart, comparing every attribute to yourself, while wondering if you can still continue to call yourself a feminist.

There's plenty of wisdom out there about how to get over a lost love, whether you ditched them or they dumped you, but here's what's worked for me.

1. Fake it 'til you make it

'What break-up? I've always been single,' you cheerily announce to your nearest and dearest. Now is the time to *Eternal Sunshine of the Spotless Mind* yourself and simply deny, deny, deny. Whenever someone mentions your partner, a simple 'who?' should suffice. Some call this the denial stage of grief, but me? What grief? Nothing happened.

2. Focus on the bad

If you must think about your ex, try to just remember all the bad things. And if they were great, just make stuff up. Tell yourself they trashed your car, gave you pink eye, stole all your money and made your body think it didn't have bowels. What a hooligan!

3. Read through old messages

I know a lot of people advise against this, but the key is to go back through everything ready to cringe. It's not romantic, it's horrific. You actually said this stuff? To a practical stranger? Gross. Delete it all and repeat Step 1.

4. Cut your hair

Past lovers stay trapped in the knots of your hair. I don't know if that's true or not, but it sounds like something they'd say in a fairy tale written exclusively for depressed women. Hair becomes tangled and so do relationships, so it's a symbolic severing of your ties to that which does not serve you to simply lop both off. Don't go overboard though. The trick is to cut off enough for compliments, but not so much that it reads as a cry for help.

5. Curate the 'gram

Breaking up is all about winning and losing, and if you're not seeing each other on a daily basis, the only portal into each other's new lives is Instagram. Hire yourself as your own social media manager and curate the hell outta your feed. Everything must scream, 'I'm over you, and furthermore, I'm having the best time of my entire life.' Every time you're standing even remotely near to someone, take a picture that makes it look like you're on a date with them, so your ex starts to feel insanely jealous. Risky? Sure. Will it work? Maybe!

Now for the small print:

Please don't take this advice. I'm terrible at break-ups and I've got no idea what I'm talking about.

Brain vs Uterus

I spend a lot of my time worrying about what would happen if I suddenly found out I was pregnant. After all, I've watched enough noughties MTV shows to know that teen pregnancy almost always ends with the girl being left to parent alone, while feeling overwhelmingly stressed trying to balance every area of her life. My parents would probably have no choice but to adopt the baby as their own, and I would spend the next 18 years arguing with my sibling/child about things like who gets the top bunk (her) or who shat on the carpet (me). On their 18th birthday, I'd finally reveal that I – still devastatingly young and beautiful – was their real mother all along. They'd understand, of course, but they'd resent me. The trauma of it all would cause them to become one of the greatest Instagrammers of our time, and they'd end up being much more popular online than me, which would, of course, be awful.

Did I mention that I'm 29?

Some people (like my entire friendship group, parents

and most of society) might argue that 29 is a perfectly reasonable age to have a baby, but not me.

> UTERUS: If anything, it's a bit late! We should start trying right now. Giving birth is one of the most joyful and exciting things a person can do.

> BRAIN: Remember the film *Alien*, where the alien bursts out of Sigourney Weaver's chest – it's exactly like that, but from your vagina.

> UTERUS: Hey! Childbirth is beautiful!

This is a constant battle between Brain, Uterus and I. Uterus wants a child, of course. It's her life-long dream, it's what she was made for, and I want to let her, but only when the time is right. And Brain has always had the perfect reason why it's not a good idea:

Age 16: Still at school
Age 17: Very bad driver
Age 18: Can legally buy Lambrini
Age 19: Saving up for summer holiday in Kavos
Age 20: Would put a real dampener on sex life
Age 21: Opportunity to be drunk in all 50 states of the USA
Age 22: Too weird
Age 23: Too fun
Age 24: Financially irresponsible
Age 25: Big birthday
Age 26: Too selfish

Age 27: Mentally unstable
Age 28: Bridesmaid for a friend (at 28 does this make her a child bride?)
Age 29: Killed too many 'unkillable' plants
Age 30: Thirty, flirty and thriving
Age 30+: Supposedly the best years of my life (why waste them by having responsibilities?)

It's a normal Sunday morning – well, afternoon – and I've woken up with a headache. For some reason, I'm craving tinned tuna, even though I don't eat fish, and I haven't had tinned tuna in over seven years. Suddenly, I need to vomit. I open my Flo app to see that my period is six days late. Six days??? I know some people have periods that pop in unannounced like a neighbour in a sitcom, but not me. I don't want to do a humblebrag, but I bleed like clockwork.

BRAIN: You're pregnant.

No. I couldn't possibly be. Could I?

UTERUS: Oh my God! Is it true? Are the rumours true?!

Maybe? I don't know. When did I last have sex? I genuinely can't remember.

UTERUS: This is amazing news! Congratulations, Mum! I'm planning the baby shower!

Hang on. I can't be pregnant. I always use condoms.

> BRAIN: Condoms are only 98 per cent effective.
> What if it was out of date? Do condoms go out
> of date? Or what if it split? Or you accidentally
> touched some of his sperm and then touched your
> vagina and did your very own private insemination?

You're right. Sperm really can infiltrate anything. I still wonder how many people have gotten pregnant with a sofa baby.

I clamber out of bed, full of adrenaline and fear, and head straight to my bathroom to do one of my 'always to hand' pregnancy tests. I stock my cabinet like a pharmacy. It's almost embarrassing how many pregnancy tests I've taken in my lifetime, especially when you consider I'm not actually having sex that frequently. With the amount of plastic I've pissed on, I should be less worried about using bags in a supermarket and more worried about hunting down bamboo-alternative pregnancy tests. At this rate, my pregnancy scares are single-handedly wiping out the entire wild turtle population.

It turns out I've already pissed away my stash of tests. I think back to last month, when I was worried that I was napping a lot because I was growing a small bean in my uterus. Or the month before that, when I had a stomach ache and was already planning my baby's first birthday party before remembering I'd eaten an entire pot of Biscoff spread with a spoon.

UTERUS: This feels different, though. This time I'm certain we're pregnant.

BRAIN: You know what they say. When you're actually pregnant, 'you just know'.

I throw up into the toilet bowl. She's right. It's time to go to Superdrug.

As I enter the shop, the overwhelmingly bright overhead lighting pierces my retinas. I head straight to the pregnancy test section. I'm on autopilot; I know it well.

BRAIN: Everyone's looking at us! They know we've been having sex.

It's like when you hear someone tell their family they're 'trying for a baby', and everyone has to congratulate the couple, even though they've essentially just told their elderly grandparents that they're constantly raw dogging the fuck out of each other.

I browse the condoms, lube and pregnancy tests, and select five, ranging in price from 'off-peak travelcard in zones 1–6 on the underground' to '14-night stay at Disney World'. Why are pregnancy tests so expensive? I suppose it does prepare you for the cost of actually having a baby.

UTERUS: If we're spending all this money, why not throw in a bottle of champagne to celebrate?

For an organ who wants to be a mother so desperately, you do not make good choices.

I don't know why, but despite being a regular test-buyer I'm still so embarrassed that I also pick up a box of plasters, a bottle of water and some nail polish, just to dilute my basket a bit. I pray that the cashier will do me a solid and hide my pile of tests among the other items I have needlessly purchased, but instead he leaves them front and centre for the entire shop to view. I am certain the elderly lady in the line behind me made an incredibly anti-feminist remark as I left. Not wanting to consume yet more plastic, I forgo a bag and walk home with the pregnancy tests shoved up my sleeves, feeling sicker than ever.

BRAIN: Get ready for your life to be over.

UTERUS: Or just beginning! You'll be so busy with a baby you'll forget everything you did before.

BRAIN: Exactly. Forget about all of your dreams, which included being free of any commitment.

UTERUS: You'll have new dreams! Filled with tiny, screaming children. You'll finally be happy!

BRAIN: How will you even look after a kid? You can barely look after yourself.

By the time I make it back to my bathroom, I've fallen hook, line and sinker for Brain's routine. Pissing on that stick feels as scary as checking my bank balance after a pretty wavy night out on the third weekend after payday. I feel dizzy, sick and petrified of what may be about to happen. Summoning all my strength, I tear open the foil and sit on the toilet.

As a seasoned professional, I don't need to read the instructions. I do this almost weekly and have yet to fuck it up.

My piss goes AWOL, firing off into three separate streams, none of which hits the stick. I bet a man designed this. There should be a class in school that teaches you the precision pissing required to pass a pregnancy test. By the time I'm done, there's piss everywhere: on the seat, on the floor and (just about) on the stick. This is what it'll be like when I have a baby, I think, now in full despair.

I take a deep breath, put the test down on my bathroom counter and wait. It's the longest 30 seconds of my life. I try to distract myself by counting the tiles on the wall. Brain has other ideas.

BRAIN: This is it. The moment of truth. You're going to be a teen mum to a world-famous instagrammer who hates your guts.

I'm pacing, sweating and thirstier than I've ever been. My head is spinning, my forehead is damp, I feel hot all over my body, like the anxiety is trying to escape my pores. If I didn't know better, I'd think I was hungover, except . . . hang on. I AM hungover. Oh my God, I'm just hungover.

I look at the test. It's negative. Of course it's fucking negative, I was sinking tequila like I was the Titanic last night. It'd be impossible to have escaped without being sick at least once.

BRAIN: That's a shame. I actually think you'd be a great mum.

UTERUS: Well, see you next month! Fingers crossed!

I head back to my bedroom, blissfully child-free, ready for an afternoon of doing whatever child-free people do. Maybe I will buy that bottle of champagne after all! I check my bank balance. Lambrini it is.

Heart vs Vagina vs Uterus

I've woken up in a puddle of my own crusty dribble to the sound of rainfall hitting my window. It's one of those lazy Sunday mornings I love. Nothing behind me but a vague, hazy sense of regret from the night before. Nothing in front of me but, well, nothing. No plans. I'm going to spend the day watching crappy TV, drinking tea and . . .

HEART: *sigh* Wouldn't it just be so nice to have someone to cuddle up to right now?

Recently, Heart has been interrupting these quiet moments more frequently. As I lie in bed, Heart reminds me there's a spare pillow beside mine. As I turn on a film, Heart reminds me I have no one to share popcorn with. As I open a book, Heart points out I'm reading all alone, which I point out is the normal way to read, but then I feel lonely anyway.

HEART: *sigh* Can't you find a big, strong man to envelop us in a bear hug and tickle our back?

I sigh back, as I'm bored of Heart's swooning after these 'big, strong men'. But . . . maybe I should get out there.

I open my phone and scroll through my contacts for anyone worth starting a conversation with. My thought process is that if I pick up from where I left off, it's twice the reward for half the work.

Sadly, there's no one. All the guys I've ever dated are either no longer single or just not my type of person. There is no 'one that got away' in my entire dating history, just a long run of 'ones I got away from'.

HEART: *sigh* What about the apps? They're full of boys.

I don't have any dating apps on my phone. I've sworn off them. If men I don't know were to shout chat-up lines at me in the street before immediately suggesting they show me their penis, I'd just walk very quickly away from them.

HEART: *sigh* If you don't get out there, how will you ever meet our one true love?

Ah. Yes. This is a thing that Heart says a lot. It's all a bit fairy tale, but I know where she gets it from: my parents. My parents have the best relationship I've ever seen. They've been together for 39 years and are sickeningly in love. The downside of this is that every relationship I enter into is filled with this level of expectation. I have the highest hopes and the highest standards, because I want what they have. They still make each other laugh, leave each other little notes, cook for each other, and hold hands when they go on walks.

As it stands, no man has quite measured up to what it is I'm looking for, though my list is surprisingly quite short.

My wish-list for the perfect man

- Kind
- Semi-Intelligent
- Funny

Clear and simple. But sadly, I'm not the only one involved. It's a collaborative effort, and when it comes to choosing a partner, I have to contend with not only Heart, but also Uterus and Vagina.

Heart lives in a fantasy world. Heart is obsessed with romance. Heart is already imagining us in 60 years' time, holding hands, reading one book together.

Heart's wish-list for the perfect man

- Must propose to us a week after meeting
- Must shower us with love

- Must be loveable
- Must want to spend every single day with us
- Must call us ten times a day
- Must bring us flowers
- Must always tell us they love us
- Must be proud to be with us and have us in at least four grid pictures on their Instagram page
- Must dote on us
- Must want to get married and live happily ever after

Then we have Uterus. Uterus cares about one thing, and one thing only: babies. Uterus doesn't care about silly gestures. Uterus is in the lab, doing genetic testing on a man we first sniffed 15 seconds ago. Actually, maybe she's ovulating right now, that would make sense.

Uterus's wish-list for the perfect man

- Must have good genes
- Must want babies

Finally, Vagina gets a say. I hate to say it, but Vagina is really the problem here. No matter how much romance Heart wants, or how many pheromones Uterus has assessed, Vagina is horned up, and she can't think about anything else.

Vagina's wish-list for the perfect man

• Alive

HEART: *sigh* Why not just give Hinge a go?
Our prince might also be hungover and lonely
right now. What if he downloads it and we don't?
We'll miss out and be alone forever and ever and
ever and ev—

Yes, OK, I got it.

I've heard good things about Hinge. Well, good things
for a dating app, which is like saying you've heard good
things about arsenic for a poison, but my hangover takes
over and I can't resist Heart's pull. I click 'Download' –
why not. The first thing Hinge does is ask me to fill in a
profile. Sadly, I have to do this by committee.

HEART: *sigh* Say we're looking for love!

UTERUS: NO! Say we're ready for kids!

VAGINA: No, keep it casual. Say we want to bang!

These are all terrible suggestions, simultaneously too
scary, too serious and too keen. I can't even begin to imagine the weirdos I'd attract and the dick picks the latter
would bring. Instead, I fill out the three standard prompts

as wittily as I possibly can and upload four pictures of myself that I've badly cut out of group photos to imply that I have way more of a social life than I actually do.

I spend the next hour flicking through profiles, looking for someone that stands out, seems like a laugh and, most importantly, meets every single need on our list. I start with my age range and height preferences set to a very limited scale, but as the hour ticks by I gradually widen my options. At this point, I'm looking for anyone between 20 and 90, ranging from 3 feet to 17 feet.

I hit the end of possible profiles to like (depressing), so close the app and wait. Maybe I'll get at least one match by the end of the day?

VAGINA: I told you, we should have liked everyone.

By 2pm, I have four whole matches.
Ben, 29, 6ft, Self-employed

HEART: Oh wow! He sounds impressive!

Michael, 31, 5ft 11 inches, Area Manager

VAGINA: He can manage my area.

Ew, no.
Thomas, 31, 6ft 3 inches, Roofer

UTERUS: Tall. Strong. He's the one. Think of the gene pool!

Jacob, 32, 5ft 11 inches, Letting Agent

VAGINA: He can let my—

Please! Come on.

There they are. Four guys, full of potential, laid out at my fingertips. They all have pros and cons, but only one can be the lucky winner.

Suddenly, I'm in the hotseat of ITV's newest dating show: *Who Will Tickle Hayley's Back?*

On my right, three hosts: Vagina, Uterus and Heart. To my left: a glitzy purple wall with light bulbs dotted along its edge. On the other side of that wall sit Ben, Michael, Thomas and Jacob. I fire questions at them one by one and whittle down the answers I'm looking for.

Three questions deep, I establish Michael has lied about his height on his profile: he's 5ft 10.5 inches, not 5ft 11 inches. So essentially a munchkin.

It's down to Ben, Thomas and Jacob. So far, Vagina would happily accept all three, she's not picky.

VAGINA: They're all breathing – I say we try them all!

Uterus bins Ben, who said he wants children but not for at least five years, which apparently is far too long for her to wait. So it's just Thomas and Jacob left. Heart is already in love with both of them. Between replies, she's googling wedding dresses and venues available for spring next year. It's down to the final decision, and the room is heated.

> HEART: Oh please, Thomas is a roofer! Swoon, what a heart throb!

> VAGINA: Imagine what he can do with those big, strong hands – send him the aubergine emoji!

Oh for goodness sake, at least act a little coy.

> UTERUS: A roofer?! No. Absolutely not. He may have good genes, but do you know how dangerous that is? Do you WANT to end up alone again?

I guess that's decided. Jacob is our guy. We talk for hours back and forth, and I find myself grinning at his replies. Finally, just as I'm about to settle down for bed, Jacob sends the message we've all been waiting for: Would love to grab a drink with you. Fancy meeting at The Bishop on Wednesday? x

I contain my excitement, before replying: Sounds good x

> VAGINA: We're in! You better get me prepped and ready. To the salon!

I arrive for the date exactly ten minutes late. I don't want to seem too keen, but I also don't want him to think I've stood him up, so this is the happy medium.

Walking into The Bishop alone to meet what is essentially a stranger feels intensely embarrassing, I feel like I've been stripped naked and everyone is looking at me. After poking my head round corners like a startled meerkat, I finally spot Jacob and give him an awkward little wave.

I find meeting new people hard at the best of times, but when that new person could potentially be your person, that's the worst. As I go in for a handshake, he dives for a hug. We both try to kiss each other on the cheek, at which point I graze his crotch while he licks my ear. Anthropologists studying us would be delighted by this bizarre mating ritual.

HEART: OK, he's even more handsome in person. Blush loads! Seriously, turn bright red now or he won't know we're literally in love already.

VAGINA: Tell him to pack his things, he's scored.

After a few drinks, it's going pretty well. He really is handsome, and funny too, with nice eyes and a good smile.

HEART: He's the one. Tell him 'I do!'

VAGINA: Drag him home. Tonight, we feast.

Our conversation is mostly light, but we also speak really openly about what we want. I tell him I'd like to eventually settle down, have a couple of kids . . .

UTERUS: Ten kids.

. . . and he replies that he wants to settle down and have a family too.

UTERUS: He's perfect. Bin the condoms, we're going in!

Uterus, Vagina, Heart and I huddle in the bathroom and agree – this guy is *it*.

After our third round of drinks we decide to call it a night. He says he has to catch the bus home, while I have a short walk back to mine. We hug goodbye and he gives me a little kiss on the cheek. I can't believe it was that quick, that easy. He's The One. We've found him. Back tickles here we come.

I watch my future husband walk away. Ahead of him, his bus rolls up to the stop and he breaks into a little jog. Just as he reaches the door, the bus pulls away, leaving him behind. He ran for a bus that didn't stop . . . I get the Ick.

BRAIN: Wow! Absolutely not. How embarrassing. Delete his number immediately.

Oh well, maybe next time.

How to Enter a Room like a Normal Person

Whenever I've organised to meet someone at a café, restaurant, pub or any other indoor venue, ideally I need them to meet me at the door and hold my hand as I enter. This is extremely uncomfortable if it's a business meeting, but needs must.

I don't want to be difficult about going into new places, but for some reason it's the most embarrassing sensation I've ever experienced. When I head into a room on my own, my cheeks burn red, as I can't help but imagine that everyone is staring at me. Scanning for my friend and/ or colleague, I feel as though I'm being watched like a hawk by a sea of judgemental eyes. They're all secretly laughing at me, wondering if I've been stood up. 'Look at that sad, pathetic loser,' they're saying to their friends, all under the guise of carrying on a perfectly normal conversation.

I should say, I've never once actually been stood up. I don't know where I got this fear from, but if I start digging down into all my irrational worries, we'll be here all day, and you don't want to hear about *all* my issues.

After many years of going places, I've put together a handy 'How To' guide on entering rooms like a pro. Gone are the days of feeling panicked, alone and afraid. Allow me to hold your hand (metaphorically) as you head into any and all of these troubling situations. You're welcome!

Entering a pub to meet a date

Whether it's a first date or a last, there is a simple one-size-fits-all solution to dealing with this entrance: have three shots of tequila before you leave the house and get there already pissed. At the door, if you can't immediately see your date – either because they're not there yet, the room is too busy, or you're just a lightweight so your eyes are already blurry – head straight for the bar. The bar is the heart of the pub. It's the safe zone! When you're at the bar, you're always busy, or at least you can pretend to be. Have another cheeky scan of the room, maybe send an 'are you here?' text, and then get to ordering another drink. Make it complicated, just to kill time – a double Long Island Ice Tea, no tequila, extra vodka, stirred not shaken please! The bartender will hate you, you'll also hate your drink, but just take the hit.

If your date hasn't arrived before your drink does, simply slam it back and order another. By now, you'll be feeling incredibly confident and drunk, two things you really need to be in this situation. Sure, you got here on your own, but maybe you'll leave with someone new?

Entering a café to meet an old friend

Don't raw dog reality on this one – walking into a café is surprisingly intense. Alcohol is almost never served in cafés, meaning you can't rely on the other customers being so drunk they don't notice your humiliating entrance. I'd recommend donning a pair of sunglasses – who cares if there's a torrential downpour, you're a star on the rise – and plugging in your headphones. Just make sure you're not actually playing any music, so that way you still have the power of your ears. When you get inside, tilt your head towards your phone so it looks like you're engrossed in a message, but instead of actually looking at your phone, let your eyes scan the room for your buddy.

If they aren't there, head straight for the toilets and hide out for at least ten minutes. People will think you've got an upset stomach, but who cares? At least they won't be laughing at you because you're a loser.

Entering a bar to meet a group of work friends

Prior to attending any work event, you should have established a favourite work friend. This is your safety pal for the night. Also, be organised. Make sure you've already checked out the venue. Make a mental note of where the room ends. Are there any dark spots? Is there more than one floor? These are the things you must establish prior to the big day. On the day of the event, before you arrive, you must text the safety pal to check that they're already there.

Ask for details about where exactly they're sitting, what they're wearing and who else is in attendance. Then, just in case, tell them you forgot your contact lenses or got stung in the eye with a stinging nettle. This gives you a good excuse if you don't spot them immediately, although it might mean you have to maintain a squint all evening (worth the risk).

Before you step over the threshold, mutter to yourself, 'I'm a bad business bitch' three times. Ideally, your boss sees your powerful, confident entrance and you are immediately promoted to CEO of the company.

Entering a restaurant to meet your partner's family

They've made you come on your own to meet their family for the first time? Break up with them. They should never let you go into that situation alone. Prick.

Everyone is far too concerned about what they are doing to notice you. You're safe.

Sex Positions for Anxious People

Sex on TV and in films has always looked so . . . wild. Two people writhing around in a rhythmic way looking incredibly sweaty and athletic. Sex has never looked like that for me. I tried having sex in the shower once. I spent most of the time away from the running water feeling incredibly cold and looking like a drowned rat. In the end, I almost knocked myself out on the valve. I'd definitely need a sturdier shower mat than mine to ever attempt it again.

I used to love looking at the sex positions in *Cosmopolitan* magazine. You know the ones – they're variations on the same four moves: you on top, them on top, standing up, and then something I'm calling 'the pretzel', which I'm sure only a professional contortionist could manage.

As a self-confessed anxious person, I've never had the confidence to suggest to a potential sexual partner that we try one of these wacky set-ups. That is, until I thought of a couple that could actually work for me.

Danger in the Dark

Some people think turning the lights off during sex is kind of boring, but personally I find it way more relaxing. There's no need to worry about your sexual partner seeing you from an unflattering angle (four chins, anyone?), and any unusual body noises can be covered up with a scared-sounding, 'What was that?'. In this move, I tell all my sexual partners in advance that my room is haunted by a queefing poltergeist. Following a queef, we both hide, terrified, under the covers together.

Go Deep

Massively successful musician Sting was famous in the 90s for telling the world he liked tantric sex, which mostly consisted of staring into his hot wife's eyes and doing a lot of deep breathing before (apparently) having the most mind-blowing orgasms of his life. I'm not into too much eye contact (terrifying, awkward and far too intimate for my liking), so in my version you trigger a mild panic attack (easily done, I just think about that weird chest pain I sometimes get, convince myself it could be a heart attack and we're in), forcing your partner to encourage you to, 'Take a few deep breaths.' Deep breathing is one of the best ways to calm down, so you'll both be asleep in no time, and I think we can all agree that a good night's sleep is, in many ways, much better than sex.

Primal Scream

Some people make a lot of noise during sex – just ask all my flatmates at uni. It was like being at a Christmas carol concert – they'd even harmonise. I reckon our neighbours loved us. This position uses sex as an excuse to have a really good scream. Seriously, just scream. You'll feel amazing. Partner and sex optional.

Dirty Talk

In this move, you describe everything in your house that needs a really good, deep clean, and then your partner helps you deal with it. It's like they say – two hands are better than one (for vacuuming and mopping the floor).

The Pretzel

Try it. I dare you. It's so complicated, you literally won't be able to think about anything else. Be sure to refer back to the queefing poltergeist, as I can assure you this position will absolutely summon her.

Baby Name Ideas based on My Primary School Classmates

At 29, I'm one of the last of my friends without children. I know, teen pregnancy really is on the rise (they're all 26+). I'm happy for them, of course, and it's great to spend time with these cute miniature humans without any of the associated responsibilities. Obviously, I sometimes think about having my own, and of course Uterus is constantly pestering me to make use of her. Though I feel no immediate urge to introduce that level of responsibility into my life just yet. But if I wanted someone to cry and shit themselves in my vicinity, I'd do it myself – I'm sure I'd be very good at it.

I do, however, love to discuss baby names with prospective parents. My favourite hobby is throwing in something completely ridiculous, like, 'What about "Plant" for a girl or "Massive Attack" for a boy?', and watching my friends try to handle it politely, while silently demoting me from Auntie status. I get it – picking a name for a child is such a big decision. It's literally with them for life, plus you have to be able to shout it confidently when you're out in public.

Choosing just one word that expresses everything about what someone is or could be is hard. Most people use a baby-name book to get a feel for what a name might say about their future child's temperament and demeanour, but I thought I'd go one step further and analyse these names in practice. Without further ado, here's a list of baby names based on the personalities of kids at my primary school:

LUKE: Bad at swimming, great at faking illness. Can start a nosebleed on cue. Always has to use the lost property PE kit, loved by all.

KIMBERLEY: Baton twirler. Gorgeous hair. Loves Great Yarmouth, all the boys fancy her.

CHARITY: Will never share her pencils but will always ask to borrow yours and never give them back. Doesn't live up to her name.

REBECCA: Great at putting crayons into small holes – ears, nose . . . you know the rest.

EWAN: Very good at art but considers it uncool so instead decides to focus on being only medium-good at tag rugby. Also spits a lot and gets in trouble to win friends' approval.

EMMA: Bases her entire personality on 'having

an older sister'. Gets pregnant at 15 (calls baby Plant), moves to hot country at 20 and lives in nature with Plant, surrounded by plants.

POLLY: Will stuff a small toy up her nose, get it removed, and immediately do it again.

JAKE: Nudist. Will always have willy out during silent reading.

LEE: Always has great snacks in his lunch box, but will never get involved in the table snack swap.

MASSIVE ATTACK: Coolest kid in school. Absolute legend, everyone's friend, nobody's enemy. Couldn't recommend this name more.

Brain vs Flying

Ah, holidays . . . Is there anything better than taking time off from real life to flop on a lounger, toes (perfectly shaved) bathing in the sunshine, thinking about nothing? Show me a better way to reset than spending a week or two in another country, sun shining, cocktail in hand, with no obligation to make your own bed. Heaven. The only problem is, no matter how hard I try, I cannot leave irrational, overthinking Brain at home, so holidays are never quite as relaxing as I'd like them to be.

> BRAIN: If anything, holidays are a great time to get some worrying done. For example, I wonder who's noticed all those razor bumps and ingrown hairs on our bikini line?

All I really want to do is take a holiday from Brain. It doesn't have to be a luxury adventure, just a short trip down the road without her warning me that a bird could shit on my head, or that every single person is judging my outfit. Instead, she is always with me, inescapable, making even the most mundane tasks difficult.

BRAIN: Hey! I'm just trying to help! But really, you *should* think about that outfit, those shoes with that pair of jeans . . . you look like a complete tit and everyone is laughing at you.

On holiday I do everything I can to escape her. I try reading, but the second I start she's like an annoying stranger who won't stop talking at you no matter how much you politely ignore them. I have to re-read every page about seven times, as Brain constantly natters in my ear, which leads to me feeling paranoid that everyone is watching me thinking, 'God, she's a slow reader, isn't she.' I am, but I don't want anyone to know that.

I've tried drinking alcohol, but then Brain forces me into humiliating decisions and spends the next day filling me with a sense of doom about what I did or didn't do while under the influence. Meditating is just as bad as reading, with none of the fun of drinking. In fact, the only thing that has ever semi-worked was when I went scuba-diving. Plunged into a freezing cold tank wearing a wetsuit and goggles, with nothing to focus on but my own breathing and the water around me, Brain was temporarily dazed into silence. Sadly, becoming a professional deep-sea diver just isn't a sustainable lifestyle choice for me.

BRAIN: Think about the hair-washing schedule.
How could we factor that into our life? We'd have
to wash it every day, plus we'd have to throw all our
clothes away to make room for the wetsuits.

So if I want to go on holiday, it always has to be with Brain
in tow, even though she's a terrible travel companion. Her
bad behaviour starts before I've even booked a trip.

BRAIN: Hello, and welcome to Hayley's Escapes,
an incredibly unreliable travel agency run by me,
Brain.

Right, well, I'd like to go on holiday. One ticket to chill
town, please!

BRAIN: Great idea, let's look tomorrow. I can't
be bothered today.

No, we're looking now. Come on, this is fun! We get to
go away!

BRAIN: Fine. What are we looking for?

Something simple, not too expensive, we just need some
sunshine.

BRAIN: Have you thought about going on a little
honeymoon in the Maldives? It's £31,000.

Honeymoon? What? I'm single. And £31,000 — are we selling a kidney to go on holiday?! I said not too expensive. Maybe I should also add realistic.

> BRAIN: Gotcha. What about a budget hotel on the Isle of Wight for ten days.

The Isle of Wight? Like . . . where my parents live? Why would I stay in a hotel, I literally have a bedroom at their house?

> BRAIN: Alright, something further away. I'm thinking New Zealand!

Right. For how long?

> BRAIN: Uh, three days.

But it takes 24 hours to get there!

> BRAIN: Oh, you want me to plan your transport, too? I know, let's go by bike.

I fire Brain as my travel agent and book a trip to join my friends for ten days in Mexico. Brain seems happy enough. I've heard Mexico is beautiful, plus going on holiday with my best mates is a much better option than going anywhere with just Brain and me. I feel chill.

That is, until a week before the trip, when Brain starts working overtime as my personal assistant.

BRAIN: Why haven't you packed? The flight is in 7 days, 4 hours and 32 minutes!

Come on, that's ages away. If we pack now we'll have to keep taking things out of the suitcase so we can wear them.

BRAIN: If you don't start straight away, you might forget something. We need to be organised.

Fine. I pull out my suitcase and head to my wardrobe. It's going to be 30 degrees, so I know I'm going to be wearing shorts or dresses every day. I pull out seven dresses, five tops, four pairs of shorts and two skirts.

BRAIN: Are you kidding? That's nowhere near enough.

I check to see if the Airbnb has a washing machine. It does.

BRAIN: Don't mess around here. If the trip is ten days, you need 20 outfits, so we have something for every day and every night, plus something to travel there and back in.

I don't own 20 outfits.

BRAIN: What about knickers?

Oh yeah, knickers! I pack ten pairs.

BRAIN: Sorry, ten?

One per day, and then I either wash them or just wear different bikini bottoms the rest of the time.

BRAIN: Oh my God, I cannot work under these conditions. You really think ten pairs of knickers is enough?

Yes . . . I mean, isn't it?

BRAIN: We need at least 30 pairs. What if we shit ourselves twice a day?

Why would I shit myself once, let alone twice a day? Plus, even if I do, there's a washing machine. But now you've said it . . . I squeeze every pair of knickers I own into my case and zip it up. It might not be the 30 pairs Brain would like (who even owns that many pants?), but at least I'm prepared if I do shit myself.

The night before I leave is when I realise just how awful at travelling Brain really is. It's 11pm and I'm tucked up in bed. My flight is at 11am, so I know that if I get up at 6am to leave for the airport by 7am, everything will be completely fine. Just as I'm dozing off, ready to dream of sunbeds and sandy toes, I hear . . .

BRAIN: Did we pack enough knickers?

Yes, we packed enough knickers. We've packed enough knickers for everyone on the trip, with spares.

I close my eyes, determined to get my seven sweet hours of pre-flight rest.

BRAIN: Did we set an alarm?

Of course we set an alarm, we always set an alarm.

BRAIN: You can't just set one! What if we sleep through it?

I have never in my whole, entire life slept through an alarm, but just to keep Brain happy, I set back-ups for 6.02am, 6.04am, 6.06am, 6.15am, 6.20am and 6.45am. The only way I'll stay unconscious through that is if I'm dead.

BRAIN: Ooh, are we worrying about death now? Now you've mentioned it, our heart does feel a bit weird, doesn't it?

No, nothing is wrong with our heart, we aren't worrying

about death right now. We have to go to sleep now so we can be well rested. Go to bed.

I put my head on my pillow and finally doze off.
   Suddenly, I'm jolted awake.

   BRAIN: Wake up! We've missed our flight! This is a disaster!

No! How is that possible? What happened to all the alarms? I clamber around trying to find my phone in the pitch-black room. I tap the screen and see the time: 2.15am. I've been asleep for less than three hours. I still have four hours until I need to wake up. We have absolutely not missed our flight, nor our alarm. I lie back down and fall asleep again.

   BRAIN: Wake up! Wake up right now!

I lurch awake. I check my phone. It's 3.30am.

   BRAIN: How many chargers did we pack?

This repeats every hour until daylight. Brain nudges me awake, wondering if the apartment will have a kettle, if the flight will be full, or if I packed enough boxes of tampons, even though I just finished my period, so it won't start again until we're home. Even Bladder gets involved, and I fumble to the bathroom with my eyes closed, desperately trying to stay sleepy enough to snooze off again.

At 6am, the alarm blares. Now Brain is exhausted from keeping me awake all night.

BRAIN: Pleeeeaaaase, just ten more minutes!

My eyes feel like they've got weights attached to them, dragging them down towards my chin. The light is burning holes in my retinas. I shower, eat a banana, pack the last-minute items I remembered in the middle of the night, and leave the flat. In true Hayley fashion, I overestimate my journey by 30 minutes – noting that I could have had an extra 30 minutes in bed – and arrive at Heathrow airport before bag drop has even opened, and obviously long before my friends.

Airports put Brain on edge. She starts getting worried, nit-picking the little things.

BRAIN: I wonder if our bag is unique enough. What if we can't remember what it looks like on the other side? Do you think everyone will have the same bag as us?

Well, it's bright pink, and it has a big label on it that says my name and address.

BRAIN: But what if you forget what colours are? Plus, you can't even see the name, it's inside a flap. We should have covered our case in bright stickers to make sure we can spot it. We need to find stickers immediately.

My friends arrive and we head over to the desks. I finish self-check-in and hoist my bag onto the conveyor belt. To be fair, I don't really feel responsible enough to check in my own luggage, I'm not even sure why the airport has this option – are any of us qualified to be doing this unsupervised? I really feel like someone should have done this for me, there's no way I've done it right. I wave my bag goodbye with the unshakeable feeling that all the knickers I own will soon be flying off to South Africa, while I land in Mexico, pant-less.

> BRAIN: You should have put a spare pair of knickers in our hand luggage.

Damn, Brain is right, but she couldn't have mentioned it before now? Still, at least underwear is something you can buy anywhere in the world.

In the line for security, something about Brain changes. As annoying as she is, she's usually pretty chatty, but here, she's the one who seems anxious. As we edge closer to the metal detectors, she finally pipes up . . .

> BRAIN: You have a kilo of cocaine in your arsehole.

I'm sorry, what?

> BRAIN: Bloody hell, stop making it so obvious. Unclench your cheeks or they're going to do a cavity search and you'll be arrested.

I absolutely do not have a kilo of cocaine in my arsehole.

BRAIN: Yes you do, and you have a gun in your bag.

A gun? I've never even touched a real gun. I do not have a gun.

BRAIN: You accidentally put one in there this morning. All of us are going to be detained, even your friends, and no one will ever forgive you.

Oh for goodness sake, this is outrageous, we are fine, we don't have anything to hide.

BRAIN: Well, I hope you're ready to be butt-fingered.

I don't want to be butt-fingered at 8.30am. I don't want to be butt-fingered at the best of times, but by a stranger, with a cold, lubed-up, gloved finger, in the middle of a crowded airport? That's no way to start a holiday. Approaching the conveyor belt, I place my hand luggage into the tray, feeling smug about how efficiently I'd divided up my items, and watch it move towards the scanner.

BRAIN: This is it. Get ready. I hope you like prison food.

Somehow I pass through security without being noticed.

BRAIN: Well done for smuggling the drugs through.

BUTT: Nah, bro, there's nothing up here.

Phew. I got too caught up in the moment. I am not a drug lord. I remove the hood from my head, try to look a little less shifty and start to relax into conversation with my friends. We roam around shops that we would never go into in real life, before buying a huge bottle of water that I'll probably down within five minutes. Then I'll spend the entire flight rushing up and down the aisle, petrified that other passengers will think I'm trying and failing to find someone to join the Mile High Club with me.

On the plane, Brain obviously tells me over and over again that we're going to die. This is old news. A bit of turbulence? Death is imminent. Our landing is delayed? This is the end. Dodgy-tasting tomato juice? Say your prayers, it's time to die. Brushing my teeth in the aeroplane sink? We are definitely going to get E.coli. I tune her out as my friends and I down miniature bottles of prosecco while planning our first night out in Mexico.

By the time we arrive in Mexico, it's late, Brain is exhausted, and she's really kicking off. We get to the Airbnb and decide we're going to crash straight away. She's livid. I've never seen her so mad.

BRAIN: Look at this place, this is a disaster.

Oh no, I think, I've made a terrible mistake. I should just have cycled to New Zealand like Brain wanted. Every time I try to do a nice thing, I blow it. I'm going to have ten days of constant stress because Brain hates every-thing. I don't know what her problem is, though – the place is lovely. I spot the kettle. At least there's a kettle, even though Brain won't want to drink anything hot while we're in a hot country. We all shotgun our beds. I lie down on the bed I've chosen . . .

BRAIN: It's too hard!

. . . turn off the lights . . .

BRAIN: They're too bright! And too dark!

. . . and try my best to fall asleep.

In the morning, the light rolls in and I wake up on my dreamy, plumped pillows. The smell of holiday is in the air. I'm well rested and all the girls are starting to wake up. I can see a sliver of sunshine pouring onto the tiled floor. I pull myself out of bed and walk to the balcony, ready to feel the heat of the day. We all sit there chatting away about how fun this holiday is going to be.

BRAIN: Wow! This is amazing and this Airbnb is to die for! We should definitely do this more often.

In fact, I say we quit our job and start travelling the world – who needs to earn money anyway? We'll just live off the land, bathe in the sea and sing for money. I know you can't sing to save your life, but maybe someone will pity us?

Buying a Coffee

I love going to cute coffee shops to pick up a hot drink. It always makes me feel grown-up, like doing my taxes, or forgetting to do my taxes.

The only issue is, like many 'hot' girls, I am extremely intolerant to dairy. This shouldn't be a problem, as we're living in what many are calling the Nut Milk Renaissance, but for some reason it is. Asking for non-dairy milk in a coffee shop that proudly announces it provides non-dairy milk is still like cracking the Enigma Code – they really, really want to end WW 2 / make you a latte, but they simply have no idea how. It is hell on earth.

Every coffee shop interaction I have goes exactly like this:

ME: 'Hello, can I get a chai latte with oat milk, please?'

BARISTA: 'Sure, a chai latte, is that for here or to go?'

ME: 'With oat milk? To go, please.'

So far, so good. The barista tells me it's £50, or however much a coffee in London costs these days. I tap my phone on the little white scanny thing and step to the side to wait. Keeping one beady eye on the barista, I see him reach for the cow's milk. I lean in.

ME: 'Hi! Sorry, just checking that's with oat milk.'

He glares at me. He checks the print-out he just made from the till.

BARISTA: 'I don't think this one's yours.'

I look around. There is no one else in the coffee shop. Perhaps he's just making himself a little coffee to give him the energy to make my drink. It makes sense – he probably has to milk those oats himself. I watch him tip chai into a metal canister. He steams the milk, delicately pours it first in one side and then the other, and adds a dusting of cinnamon. Then he hands it to me.

I stare at the drink.

ME: 'I'm so sorry, I think mine was with oat milk.'

He looks at me in disgust. What have I done? How have I wronged him? Maybe he's being held hostage and he's trying to send me a signal. Shit, I've ruined his life.

BARISTA: 'The chai latte, right?'

He's so certain he wants to give it to me that he puts on a lid and offers it up again. I can already feel my stomach gurgling. I don't know what to do. I hold out my hand and accept the milky drink.

ME: 'Thank you so much.'

I leave the coffee shop and immediately put it in the bin. Thank God there are coffee shops everywhere now. Let's try again. I take out my card, stride into the next one, and order.

ME: 'Hello, can I please get a chai latte with oat milk?'

BARISTA: 'Sure, a chai latte, is that for here or to go?'

How to Defeat Imposter Syndrome

I've got this one shit friend who insists on coming everywhere with me. Her name is Imposter Syndrome and she's the worst. She's a complete arsehole and thinks I'm terrible at everything. She can do it all (obviously) — she's a jack of all trades and a natural overachiever. She has perfect hair that looks great even unbrushed (of course), wears sky-high heels without so much as tripping, and always wears a bold red lip that if I did the same would make me look like I'd eaten roadkill. She's everything I'm not and *loves* to remind me of that fact.

Recently, I decided that I was sick of dealing with Imposter Syndrome on my own, so I decided to recruit some help. He's a straight, white male, and while he won't show me his credentials, he's positive he can help me sort her out. His name is the Guru. His rates are through the roof (he claims they reflect his worth), so I decide to give him a trial for one day.

At the coffee shop

It's 8.30am and I'm picking up a chai latte with oat milk (fingers crossed) before work, when Imposter Syndrome butts in right next to me. She never stands in line; apparently, she deserves to be at the front. She eyes up my order.

> IMPOSTER SYNDROME: Only cool
> girls drink chai lattes, who are you trying
> to fool?

Before I can reply, Guru steps in to advise.

> GURU: Don't listen to her. Stand your ground.
> Who is she to say you're not cool? Are you even
> trying to be cool with your drink choices? I don't
> think so. Plus, you've earned another stamp on
> your loyalty card, so the universe will soon reward
> you with a free latte.

Guru is right. I pick up my chai latte – which I drink because it tastes delicious and I can't drink coffee – then stride out of the coffee shop as Imposter Syndrome runs after me. Bad day to be wearing such high heels, bitch.

At the office

I've made it to work. It's the start of the week and, as the social media manager, I have to delegate tasks to the rest of my team. Suddenly Imposter Syndrome is sitting at my desk beside me.

> IMPOSTER SYNDROME: You? Delegating tasks to a team? Give me a break! You can't even load the dishwasher properly. No one will listen to you.

On my other side, Guru appears.

> GURU: Don't even think about it. If you speak with conviction, look serious, make a couple of jokes so everyone knows you're a nice person, and then tap, tap, tap away on your silly little computer all day, no one will question your authority.

I'm on the clock with Guru, so I follow his advice. I have a great day at work, get all my tasks done, and don't even think about the fact that I still have no fucking idea how to use Excel.

On a hot date

After work, I've got a date planned with Tom, a guy I've been chatting with. He's handsome, like, *really* handsome, possibly too handsome – where are his flaws? As I get to the pub and spot him leaning against the bar, Imposter Syndrome leans in next to me.

> IMPOSTER SYNDROME: Oh, he is way out of your league. I wonder if he's doing this as a dare. Everyone in here probably thinks he's your brother – either that or you're a pity date.

I turn to leave, but Guru blocks the way.

> GURU: He's seen your photos, so he must think you're at least a bit attractive, but maybe he's not even that shallow. Perhaps he wants to find a genuine human connection, or even just have a bit of fun. Get in there and get to know each other. Even if it isn't right, you might meet a new friend.

He gives me a push, and I stride confidently towards the bar. Tom looks up at me and smiles, so I smile back. He asks me what I want to drink, and I tell him I'll have a gin and tonic. I expect Imposter Syndrome to pop up and tell me that's a drink for hot girls, and I'm just a little worm, but she's nowhere to be seen.

I scan the room, and there, in the back corner, Imposter Syndrome and Guru are making out. Well, that's one way to keep her busy, I guess.

Safe Conversation Starters

I'm not great when it comes to meeting new people, Brain has me second-guessing myself constantly, making me a socially awkward mess in new settings. Heading into a room full of new people is where Brain and her anxious chatter thrives. She often makes me feel as though I have nothing interesting to say, and usually I'm so worried about what they'll think of me, and so consumed in Brain's chatter, to even think about how I should start a conversation.

Of course, it's all about small talk. If we could collectively wipe one thing from the reality of human existence, I think we can all agree it'd be small talk. Yes I know what you're thinking – what about all the horrifying stuff that happens in the world, and all the hunger? Well, that too, but awkward small talk is the next priority.

Other than avoiding dairy and constantly worrying about being pregnant, having to make small talk is basically one of Brain's biggest concerns. To combat this I've compiled a list of three useful conversation starters that take at least some of the stress out of chatting to people you don't really know.

1. Talking to a stranger

If, for some wild reason, you need to start a conversation with a stranger – say you've been paired with them in a team-building exercise or you're trapped together in a mine – always start with a compliment. Avoid anything too intimate like, 'You have really nice eyes', unless you're genuinely trying to hit on them. I try to start with a neutral, 'That's a jacket!' If they aren't wearing a jacket they'll think you're delusional and possibly walk away (bonus). But if they are wearing one, it's not quite a compliment, but it's not *not* a compliment either. Introduce yourself and go from there.

2. Joining a group

You're at a party and you don't know anyone, so the host drops you into a group who are mid-anecdote. This is potentially incredibly awkward, as you're already on the back foot. I recommend waiting for a break in the story, ideally after a big laugh (that you absolutely must join in on) or a loud sigh, before saying, 'So you guys have known each other for a while then?' Either they do, and they'll tell you all about it, or they don't, and they'll think you're making a hilarious meta-joke about the concept of parties and everyone will burst into laughter, and you'll go down in history as the best party guest ever.

3. At the hairdresser's

Going to the hairdresser's is a primo small-talk destination. It's the danger zone. You're completely trapped, and the other person is quite literally holding a huge pair of scissor-shaped blades next to your ears. You can't risk distracting them, but at the same time, you can't sit in silence like a serial killer planning their next move. I like to ask, 'What's the biggest hair disaster you've seen recently?' and just hope they don't say me.

Brain vs Body

I've never had a strong liking for mirrors – they always seem to lie. Some of them make you look small, some make you look tall, and some make it look as though your eyes are about to pop out of your freakishly small pin-head that's attached to your stretched-out limbs. The latter mostly happens when I find myself in 'fun houses' at low-budget fairgrounds.

The relationship I have with my body has changed a lot over the years, but the one thing that has stayed consistent is the fact that Brain has always found fault with my body. She's told me my arms are too big, my legs are covered in too much cellulite (possibly the most normal thing in the world), my stomach sticks out too far, my hips hang over my trousers too much, my boobs are too small, my shoulders are weird . . . the list goes on and on.

It's never been fun looking at my own reflection, and I've never been able to look at my body in the mirror without Brain telling me she hates it. I find myself wearing clothes with long sleeves to cover up my arms, baggy t-shirts that won't cling to any part of my body, and jeans that hang loosely around my legs so as not to bring attention to them. Maybe this is why I often look like Rumpelstiltskin.

My camera roll is filled with pictures of me over the years, sometimes in a bikini or underwear (cheeky), sometimes in my normal uniform, sometimes in tight dresses or holiday attire. At the time each picture was taken I remember the loathing I felt towards my body. The way Brain would torment me and tell me how disgusting I was, that I should improve the way I look. But today, as I look back through these images, I wonder how I could have possibly loathed that girl so much. I see a happy smile, a person that looks like me, only she's got a better face, a better body than the me I know today.

I open my camera app, pose in front of the mirror and take a full-length picture of myself. When I look at it all the loathing comes back, and here is Brain to nit-pick my appearance.

BRAIN: You look hideous, when did you get so old and ugly? You have to delete that, you troll.

Instead of deleting the picture, I keep it, knowing that next year that face, that body, that person will be the person next year's me will be competing with. She is the same girl today as she will be next year, so why can't I love her now?

I don't think it's easy for people to fall in love with

their bodies. For women especially, I think it's difficult growing up consuming so much in the media about how a body should look and what is considered 'unattractive'. Bodies trend just like fashion, which is fucking barbaric. Our bodies are the vessels we have with which to live and experience life, they are not and should not be treated as a fashion accessory.

We all have hang-ups about our bodies. No matter how you look, how big or small you are, Brain will always, *always* find a fault to focus on, so perhaps we shouldn't pay such close attention to her opinions.

Brain vs Presentation

I've never been very good at public speaking. When I was growing up, my parents noticed how shy I was, so my dad decided to do the obvious thing and put my brother and I on the stage. This technique was one he'd learned from his own parents: thrust them into the face of what scares them and they'll defeat the demon head on. I'm just thankful I never told him how terrified I am of sharks.

It had worked for my dad, though, who loved to tell one particular story about overcoming his fears. When he was six years old he met a dog who had a big, yappy bark. He was terrified and ran straight home, screaming. The next day, his parents showed up with two Great Danes. My dad became friends with them pretty quickly, which was good, because my grandparents went on to own 13 massive dogs. I still don't understand how that many giant dogs could possibly fit in a three-bedroom, semi-detached house, but there we are.

Little did my dad know that it wasn't going to be quite as easy to nip my seemingly irrational fear of public speaking in the bud, because he also had to deal with Brain. I don't know if you've ever tried to speak to a room full of people while your busy Brain is narrating along, but to me it feels like a challenge on *I'm A Celebrity Get Me Out Of Here*. Which is to say, I'd rather eat a kangaroo's balls.

My dad's solution was to stick my brother and I in a local theatre school called Stagecoach. If you were a child in the 90s, you might have done the same. We'd meet every Sunday in an old, definitely haunted theatre to learn dances, songs and 'acting', the idea being that by the end of it we'd be what the dance industry like to call 'a triple threat'. Every six weeks we'd hold a compilation show where we'd present snippets from popular West End musicals, performed extremely badly. Sometimes more than 500 people would come to these shows (I presume they were forcing the entire population of the Isle of Wight to fill the seats). Honestly, I'd have preferred to face 500 big dogs.

Although I went to these classes for years, I never remotely got over my fear of being on stage, and if anything also developed a terrible fear of the films *Oliver!* and *Annie*. As an adult I'm more afraid of public speaking than ever. I hate it so much, I was almost sick when I got picked on in the front row of a comedy show, and I'm literally a comedian. I prefer to air my dirty laundry on the internet, where it's nice and safe. You can't block someone in person. Trust me, I've tried many times.

Today, however, I have a presentation to do. I'm not

long out of university, and I've just started a new job at a 'cool' agency. It's full of men who all laugh at each other's jokes, and women who are much, much smarter than I am, but I'm among 11 new hires, so at least I'm not the only one who looks confused all the time. Last week, on our first day, we were told that all 11 of us had to do a presentation on something interesting about ourselves. I'm not sure why they couldn't have just done that awful thing where you stand in a circle and everyone goes round introducing themselves, telling each other one interesting fact. I always say I have one of Elton John's original paintings hanging in my kitchen. It's definitely not true, but it sure is interesting. Plus, anyone who hears it now thinks Elton John is an artist – free PR, you're welcome Elt-Jo.

Now here's something you should know about me: I take people at face value. Even at school, when my friends would say they'd barely studied for a test and then miraculously get perfect grades, I assumed it was divine intervention. Here is a list of things people have said to me vs what they've actually done:

'It's a low-key, casual wedding, just friends and family in an informal setting.' It was the biggest fucking wedding I've ever been to. Everyone was dressed like film stars. I however, looked like I'd just rocked up from a sad summer fete – and I forgot to tell my boyfriend so had to go on my own.

'I'm probably just going to wear something old that

I've already got in my wardrobe.' They had a full glam squad, a stylist, hair and make-up. I wore black jeans with a black top and had to stand at the back in photos, like I was their assistant.

'I think I'll get Tiffany an iTunes voucher for her birthday.' They got Tiffany a gold-plated necklace with her children's initials on it, along with a bunch of flowers and personalised gift wrapping. I got her a bottle of budget wine, a Terry's chocolate orange and a card from the Co-op.

With all this experience, I should have known better. I have had so many of these situations thrown at me and have been caught short every time, but my superpower is that I never learn. This time, I've spoken to everyone else about their presentations, and they've all agreed they're just going to throw something together. Zero effort, very chill, all good. We're all going to be equally underprepared, just how I like it.

The day arrives. We gather in a conference room and I notice that my name is at the very end of the list. Phew. By then, everyone will be nice and tired, so we can probably just zip through what I've got in five minutes rather than ten. I settle back with butterflies in my stomach, ready to watch my brand-new colleagues do the bareminimum, as promised.

First up, it's Alexa. She starts playing an animation she made at uni. It's incredible. It's like a mini Pixar film. At the end, everyone gives her a huge round of applause.

BRAIN: Whatever, she made it ages ago. That's
no effort at all.

Next up, it's Jesse. He seems really nervous, which makes
me feel more nervous. He talks for five minutes about
basic stuff: where he's from, what he did at uni, how he
wound up in this job. Normal, very typical 'office chat'.
Nice one, Jesse. This is exactly what I like to see. Suddenly, the lights dim and he throws a hand gesture to
Billy from accounts, who is standing behind a mixing
deck.

BRAIN: Oh shit. This seems planned.

Music starts to blare out. It's a backing track. He's rapping! He's fucking rapping. Oh my fucking God, he's
written an entire rap about his life. The rap is impeccable
and funny. The entire room is buzzing. Everyone's grinning or laughing and clapping along. His presentation is
going down like a storm. I hear people whispering about
him releasing it on Spotify.

BRAIN: OK, we should pretend we're feeling
sick and leave. This is not going to end well for us.

I look to the door, but there are too many people in
the way. The butterflies in my stomach are increasing, I
feel light-headed. If I want to pull a sicky it would have
to be the performance of a lifetime, and even with my

world-class Stagecoach training, I'm not sure I can pull it off. At the end of the rap, Jesse gets a standing ovation. The entire room goes wild and he takes a well-deserved bow, before returning to his seat next to me. He nudges me and tells me how much fun it is. According to him, I have 'nothing to worry about!'

BRAIN: Oh, we have *everything* to worry about.

The CEO is still reeling from Jesse's performance when he brings up Saeed. Saeed also nods for the lights to be dimmed, before introducing a 15-minute documentary he made – wait for it – this week.

BRAIN: Hayley, I'm not being funny, this is a code red. You need to fake your own death right now.

The documentary is incredible. It's emotional, funny and gripping. As it draws to a close, he thanks everyone and the room goes absolutely wild with noise. The CEO comes back to the stage and tells the room how proud he is to have such talented new employees as part of the team. Against the glass of the back wall, other employees from surrounding offices are also gathering to watch. News has spread building-wide.

BRAIN: Fuck. You cannot go up there now.

One after another, my fellow recruits get up and present what I can only describe as a Nobel-Prize-worthy talent show. They've made scientific discoveries, choreographed moving dance pieces, painted masterpieces, invented new technologies. The crowd are laughing, crying and high-fiving each other. Every single one of these fucks tried their absolute hardest. They lied to me.

Finally, the CEO gets up and says, 'Well, if the rest are anything to go by, I think we're in for an incredible last presentation! Please welcome to the stage, our final presenter of the day . . . Hayley Morris!'

BRAIN: This is career suicide. You can't do this. Jump out of the window.

I walk with trembling legs towards the stage to the sound of clapping, but the only thing I can hear is my heart beating in my ears. Everything is happening in slow motion. I feel sick, so incredibly sick. I'm not even sure I'm going to make it to the front.

BRAIN: Abort! Abort! You *need* to sit back down.

I finally reach for the microphone and introduce myself, even though they all just heard my name. My voice is shaking, along with my hands, and I can see everyone's eyes on me. My own blur in and out of focus. I just have to get through the next five minutes. Five minutes and then I can sit down. So what if my presentation isn't as long or as good as anyone else's? It means we all get to go to lunch earlier. Everyone loves lunch.

I nod for my PowerPoint to be pulled up onto the big screen. The crowd's eyes widen in anticipation. What wonder am I going to reveal to them? It's a fucking slide show of pictures of me in different locations in the UK. Literally just picture after picture of me on Isle of Wight beaches, standing on roads in Scotland, outside bakeries in Portsmouth and next to old cars in Brighton. I don't even have interesting anecdotes to accompany these pictures. Sometimes, I can't even remember why I took them. Why did I think this was a good idea? This makes me the talentless fuck of the office who's visited a couple of cities in the UK.

I fumble through my pathetic excuse for a presentation as, one by one, everyone in the room starts to direct their attention to their phones. I've lost them. I can't even keep Simon from HR engaged, and he's probably the most polite man who has ever lived. As I round up the presentation I announce that I'd like to be a comedian and I am practically laughed off stage.

Shortly after this, I quit my job. Mainly out of embarrassment, but also because there was another presentation coming up and I didn't have the bottle to go up there again. I reckon I'd have been dragged off stage before I even spoke into the microphone. If I could give you any single piece of advice off the back of this experience it would be this: believe no one. Oh, and always have a pre-prepared rap up your sleeve.

. . . And if you absolutely have to do a presentation/ speech or any public speaking in front of a room full of strangers, don't imagine them naked, that's weird and possibly arousing for some people. Instead, just imagine they are all your best mates; that way you can act like a tit, stumble over your words and know you are in safe, non-judgemental hands. Unless your best mates are like mine, in which case they'll ridicule you for your fuck-ups for the rest of your life.

Brain's Advent Calendar

Over the last few years I've noticed an emerging trend for fancy advent calendars. Big, extravagant-looking boxes filled with make-up samples, individual packets of tea or, if you're really avant-garde, different types of pork crackling – a very definite target audience. You can even get them for your pets. Despite not having any pets, those are the ones I most want to buy. Sadly, they're usually really expensive and I'm way too tight to spend that kind of money on miniature items. Instead, I have a completely free, unique and reusable calendar that Brain uses to hurl random thoughts at me as we move through the festive season. And I'm sharing it with you. What a treat.

1st Dec: It's December! Don't you think we should have started our Christmas shopping by now? It's only three weeks until the big day. What if there's an earthquake and you can't reach the shops? Everyone will think we hate them.

2nd Dec: Why not spend six hours online browsing socks for your brother? Socks are the perfect gift if you want to say, 'I don't understand what boys want for Christmas at all, but I very much care about the temperature of your feet!'

3rd Dec: It's time to send your Christmas cards. I realise you haven't posted a physical letter since the early 2000s, but it's extremely rude if you don't send one to your second cousin's wife's boss, for some reason.

4th Dec: Let's go and find a massive tree to put in the front room! None of that plastic stuff this year. If we get a real one, we'll be able to enjoy the delicious smell of fresh pine needles until January.

5th Dec: Oh my God, there are pine needles everywhere! It's like walking through broken glass. They're raining down like bullets every time we walk past. Where the fuck is our vacuum?

6th Dec: Text Mum and ask for a broom for Christmas. Sure, it's a boring present that will make you feel like an old lady, but at least we'll be able to cross the living room without bursting into tears.

7th Dec: It's our work Christmas party! Strap yourself into a sequinned dress and figure out who we're going to get off with in the photocopier room.

8th Dec: Greg? Really? Greg from accounts? You should be ashamed of yourself. I thought we'd at least go for someone interesting this year.

9th Dec: Sorry, I'm still thinking about the Greg thing. He's not even our type. Can I interest you in a series of flashbacks of you and Greg making out? I think it's the only way you'll see how wrong you got it.

10th Dec: What's your favourite Christmas song? Mine's 'Jingle Bells'. Shall I sing it to you, over and over again? Maybe as you're drifting off to sleep? Done.

11th Dec: Take a look at this article about how someone's Christmas tree set on fire and burned them and their entire family to death. What a desperately sad story!

12th Dec: Jingle Bells, Jingle Bells, Jingle all the waaaaaaay.

13th Dec: Friend-mas drinks tonight! We're not doing presents, are we? No one's gonna buy gifts for 15 people.

14th Dec: Well, we can never see those friends again. Hope you enjoy your thoughtful gifts, you friendless freak. You will forever be known as the bitch that got no one a gift for Christmas.

15th Dec: Jingle Bells, Jingle Bells, Jingle Bells, Jingle Bells.

16th Dec: Repeat after me – drinking mulled wine at 9am is absolutely fine and in no way indicative of a problem. Oh, a dried orange wheel, doesn't that look fancy on our glass?

17th Dec: Last day of work! Not officially, obviously, but there's no point doing anything else now. It's practically Christmas Day! It's rude to send emails in December!

18th Dec: Eating little Christmas-shaped items for breakfast, lunch and dinner is a great way to live. We should do this all year round! Life's too short to not constantly be slamming down Christmas-tree-shaped crumpets.

19th Dec: Let's watch a Christmas film! Something on Netflix maybe? Hang on, this chick has realised she's a Christmas princess 13 different times? Let's watch them all!

20th Dec: Have you bought enough presents for your mum? Better go and get some more. The important thing to remember is that Christmas is not about family or spending time with each other, it's about how much money you spend on the ones you love. That is the only way they'll know we love them. Oh, and we should probably treat ourselves to something nice as well . . .

21st Dec: OK, that new outfit looks amazing on you. Plus, I think you'll get loads of wear out of it. I've seen lots of people rocking a jumper that says, 'Hands Off My Christmas Puddings!' in June.

22nd Dec: Time to head home! How exciting! What a thrill! There's nothing better than spending six straight days with your nearest and dearest. Family is everything!

23rd Dec: OK, that's enough time with family now.

24th Dec: It's Christmas Eve! Time to start drinking. It's the Christmas spirit! Get it? Spirit, because they're spirits! Hot apple cider is . . . delicious. It's so sweet, it just tastes like apple juice. Why don't we just drink these all night?

25th Dec: Oh, that's why. Happy Christmas, why are we awake at 6am? Can you turn the cheer down? I'm going back to sleep.

A Fresh Start

I really love to watch people on YouTube do their self-care routines. It's the most satisfying thing. You know who I mean – the type of people who live in perfectly spotless all-white houses, in which every rug is fluffed to within an inch of its life, every surface is so well polished you can see your own reflection, and there are literally hundreds of Neom candles burning at all times. They make videos of themselves filling their fridges with all the snacks you could ever desire, which creates this beautiful ASMR click every time an item reaches the shelf. They spend their Sundays soaking in mounds of bubbles, doing endless face masks and making the most creative to-do lists for the week. I'd like to spend a day in their homes engulfed in that sweet, sweet smell of Neom luxury. Sadly, I'm not sure my life will ever look as warm and cosy as theirs.

I do have a self-care routine, though. It's one that I like to follow every Sunday. It's called 'Hayley's Fresh Start' and it goes a little something like this . . .

9.30am: I wake up. Rest is essential, so I aim to get loads of it. Well, not loads. I went to bed at 3.30am, so I've really only had six incredibly broken and sweaty hours. I'm stupidly hungover and my head is pounding, but luckily I remembered to take my make-up off during the night . . . using my pillowcase. I lie in bed and visualise (all the horrors from the night before – dancing on tables, talking utter nonsense to a random group of girls in the toilet, twerking like Tina Belcher at the dinner table and walking into a glass window).

2pm: I fuel my body. I've been festering in my hungover state long enough. Nutrition is everything, so I order an extra-large pizza and three bottles of Lucozade Sport. An athlete needs to hydrate. I get those muscles moving by transferring myself from the bedroom to the living room, where I lie on the sofa and watch TV while simultaneously scrolling on TikTok for the next six hours.

8pm: I've done nothing all day. I'm feeling pretty restless and start to really ponder on my life. I'm gross, aren't I? Like, really, really gross. Something's got to change. I can't go into another week like this. I'm an adult, aren't I? So why am I sat here festering like a feral animal?

8.05pm: I stand up and start clearing everything 'unhealthy' out of the cupboards. And I mean everything. I strip those cupboards bare. The biscuits go straight into the bin – though I do have one more, just to say goodbye – along with the leftover pizza. My boyfriend (that's right folks, I bagged myself a boyfriend, Simon, who's a total diamond) pokes his head around the door and asks, 'What are you doing?', so I throw a dry crust of pizza at his head. He retreats to the bedroom to hide. I guess he isn't willing to change his life yet, unlike me.

8.40pm: I clean like a demon, if a demon only owned one old cloth and an inch of bleach. Why don't I have any cleaning stuff? I have a whole drawer of dishwasher salt. I scrub the sink and even two whole drawers of the fridge. I yell at Simon that he has to remove every item he owns from the living room, but he pretends he's dead rather than having to interact with me. Classic Simon move.

9pm: I take some old vitamins that I find in a drawer. At least, I think they're vitamins. Starting tomorrow, I've decided that I'm going to eat only smoothie bowls for breakfast, lunch and dinner. I'm going to be 10 per cent woman, 90 per cent smoothie. Plus salads, obviously. I'm going to eat so many salads, there won't be any left for anyone else. Maybe I'll be like that girl who was on the news who turned orange because she ate too many carrots, except I'll probably be green because of all the leaves. Carrots suck.

9.30pm: Before getting into bed, I make a schedule for the week. Every day, I'm going to get up at 5am for yoga, meditation and hot lemon water. Yes, it tastes a little on the funky side, but everyone knows the worse something tastes, the better it is for you. I'm pretty sure that's the point. Then I'll smash it at work, every single day. In a month or so I'll probably be a team leader at whatever company it is I work for by then (I'll have been head-hunted within a week).

10pm: I start a gratitude journal in a brand-new note-book, and it feels like I'm really starting a new chapter of my life now. I start wildly listing things I'm grateful for, looking around the room wide-eyed for inspiration. I'm grateful for my curtains! I'm grateful for bin, I'm grate-ful for rug, and even my empty fruit bowl (I make a note to actually buy fruit to go in said fruit bowl). I delete all the apps off my phone. I briefly think about throwing it out of the window before turning it off and putting it in a drawer (wouldn't be very 'new me' to smash up my phone). Look at me, living a technology-free life, like my phoneless ancestors. I feel relaxed, I feel powerful, I feel brave. I can't wait to tell everyone about my healthy new lifestyle. I close my eyes, put my head on the pillow and . . .

It's Monday, 8am. I missed my 5am alarm as my phone was turned off. Oh well, I guess I'll start yoga tomorrow. I get out of bed and head to the kitchen to make some hot lemon water, but I'm out of lemons, so I grab a handful of Rice Krispies out of the bin instead. I fish my phone out of the drawer, turn it on and . . . open TikTok. By now it's 9am and I need to leave for work. The week is practically gone. Still, they always say it's best not to make big changes too quickly, don't they? I know – next Sunday can be my real fresh start.

Things My Brain Thinks
about During Sex

By now I think it's fairly obvious that Brain is very loud,
overbearing and annoying. She's constantly whittering on
about stuff I don't have any interest in thinking about and
butting in as I try to get on with my day-to-day life. Some
days she is much louder than others, and some days I'm
able to drown her out a bit better – usually when I'm
doing things I get pleasure from, like listening to music
or watching a really gripping film.

Sex? Very sadly, sex is not one of those times. I
really thought it would be the ultimate Brain silencer,
but for some reason she just gets louder and louder
in intimate moments. Thankfully she's not ruined sex
for me, but I do have to put up with her shouting over
and over in my head, which is incredibly distracting
when the whole point of sex is to very much be in the
moment. You need laser focus for the ending to be a
happy one.

I've come to the conclusion that Brain is the loudest

when she feels intimidated, not skilled enough, self-conscious or aware that complete concentration is needed. Given that sex makes Brain feel all of these things, it's no surprise that her monologue goes a little like this:

Are we supposed to be moving around more? Or moving around less?

Is he rubbing our inner thigh? Does he know that's our inner thigh

I think we're going to get friction burn, maybe we should move his hand.

Oh, OK, did you just kiss his ear?

Is it hygienic to kiss ears? I wonder when he last washed his ears properly. I bet no one cleans behind their ears as much as they should.

Just making a mental note to give our ears a really good scrub next time we're in the shower. We should buy a new loofah too! A blue one would be fun.

I think we should be making some noises now. It's a bit creepy that we're just laying here breathing into his neck. It's awkwardly quiet. Oh, what's that? You want me to shut up? I just thought that if you're not making outward noises, I should make inward noises instead?

OK, I'll be quiet now.

. . .

I don't want to alarm you, but there's a massive cobweb in the corner of our bedroom and I can't see the spider.

Oh no, do you think the spider is in the bed with us?

He's really sweating, is it normal for him to be sweating this much?

Oh my God, imagine if the spider climbed inside our vagina and laid its eggs in us? Would we technically be the mum when we give birth to the little spider babies?

I think his sweat is going to make our face spotty. You should wipe it off our cheek. We don't need any new spots to appear and ruin our weekend plans.

Woah! Steady on, sir, does he know he's diving for our arsehole?

No, he's just confused. Two holes. They only have one! Definitely confusing for them.

He wants us to go on top, doesn't he? I hate going on top. Moan more! He won't want to ruin our experience! We'll be embarrassingly out of breath if we change positions.

Did he just ask us to call him daddy? I don't think we should do that. It feels a bit odd. We'd never be able to look our dad in the eye again. Call him by his actual name.

Oh shit, we never did our laundry! We really need those cream trousers for tomorrow. I reckon if we put the washing machine on after this they'll still dry in time.

Woah, this is a new position!

I think we need to pee.

Maybe we could put the trousers on the radiator? If we put the washing machine on straight after this then we can put the heating on to dry them and they'll be dry just in time for morning.

We definitely need to piss!

Wait . . . Is he trying to get us to queef?

Wait, why is he pulling out? We're not finished yet.

How selfish of him to finish so quickly! We did so much work laying there so nicely.

Oops, someone moved too quickly! There she is! There's that queen of the vagina, queef, making her exit. Wow, what a symphony!

Well . . . We better go pop those trousers in the wash now.

How to Enjoy Sex as a Grown-Up

When you're in high school, losing your virginity is considered to be the coolest, sexiest thing you can do. It's an odd thing to be obsessed with losing, and we're somehow all brainwashed into believing it's the single most important thing that any human can do. How can we possibly become adults if we're still equipped with our 'intact cherries'?

I lost my virginity when I was 16, which I find odd now, because when I look at 16-year-olds today, they look far too young to be doing anything like that. It was an experience no one prepared me for. There I was, thinking it'd all be birds singing, harps playing, and I'd be wrapped in delicate silk linens, feeling euphoric. In reality, it was quite shit. I was tipsy off one Smirnoff Ice that I'd had for Dutch courage. It wasn't with a boyfriend but with a good friend of mine, and it fucking hurt. I couldn't understand what all the fuss was about, and why people kept telling me it was the most magical thing they had ever experienced.

The most magical thing I had ever experienced was when I was at Disney World and one of the people who worked there let me and my family ride The Tower of Terror twice in a row. This? This was like riding the tea-cups at a dodgy seaside fairground. It was disappointing and left me feeling nauseous.

Now I'm an adult, I know so much more about how to get what I want out of a sexual experience, which makes the whole thing way easier and much more fun.

Here are my top tips for great sex:

- Establish a time limit. Sometimes we don't want to go 'all night long'. Before you start, talk about a hard out time. *Bake Off* starts at eight? Get down to business at seven, but never stop talking about Prue Leith. That way, you'll both get on with it quicker than you can say, 'Are those muffins ready?'
- Clear your to-do list first. If, like me, you find it hard to concentrate on sex when you're thinking about other things (you know, like, whether those cream trousers have been washed), use this as motivation to get your minor chores done. Ideally, share this with your partner, so they can clear up their shit too! Remember: foreplay starts with a clean kitchen, freshly washed cream trousers and empty bins.
- Pick music with a manageable cadence. This is not the time for fast-paced post-punk rhythm

changes, nor is it the time to try out Reddit Guys playlist (if you know, you know, and if you don't, a quick TikTok search will clear that one up). Make sure you're not including anything that reminds you of family, previous lovers or your childhood. I recommend starting with something slow, and ending with a fast-tempo track under three minutes – no one has the stamina to thrust to a fast tempo for longer than three minutes.

- Learn to say no. You don't have to turn in an Oscar-winning performance if you're not in the mood. Say goodbye to faking a headache or a bad back and just say no. If you want to be polite, you can offer a high five or a short dance performance as you deliver your response.

Me vs Face

Acne is one of those things – like kids or a yeast infection – that you can't fully understand until you've actually lived with it. A lot of people think that when you talk about acne you're overhyping what are essentially 'spots', but from the age of 14 to 27, cystic acne was a sadistic drill sergeant who ran, and tried to ruin, my entire life.

> ACNE: Alright, cadet! Get up! School starts in two hours, what's the plan?

The second I woke up, I would touch every inch of my face to feel if any new bumps had appeared overnight and – spoiler alert – they always had. Looking down, my pillow would be covered in blood – real Sleeping Beauty stuff. Sexy. If a prince had come to wake me from my slumber with a kiss, I'd have had to be like, 'Get out! Get the fuck out!!!' until I'd had time to change my pillowcase, which I did at least five times a week.

I would then drag myself to the bathroom, where I

would conduct a close-up examination of my entire face. It's pretty impressive how bad I was at geography considering how good I was at identifying any minor topographical shift on my own skin. I knew the location of every crater and every mound. It was like studying the surface of the moon, in that if I was at a certain angle in a certain light, I was sure I could see a face.

ACNE: Clock's ticking. Hit the showers, we've got places to be!

I'd hop in the shower and use up to 15 'gentle', 'mild' or 'anti-inflammatory' face washes. The ones that were on the scratchier side felt the best. They would leave me, without fail, bright red and painfully dry. During this portion of my routine, I'd note exactly how my acne was currently dispersed: was I rocking acne sideburns? Or an acne beard? Was it all clustered around my nose? You know, the kind of fun game you play while wasting millions of litres of water. It was always the beard; I never really needed to check.

Before school, or work, or even just briefly interacting with those who knew and loved me best in the world, I would cake myself in so much make-up I'd resemble an Almond Magnum. I'd use two different concealers, foundation and almost an entire pot of translucent powder at a time. I considered whether it would shave some time off my routine to simply comb my hair straight over my face like the girl from *The Ring*, but after careful thought I realised that might make it hard to eat and I wasn't going to make myself even more miserable than I already was.

After finishing my make-up, I'd cry. I realise some women wake up early to do yoga, meditate and drink green juices, but there's almost never been a time in my life when I've woken up early to do anything other than cry at my own reflection. If I was smart, I would probably have done this before putting on my make-up, but since part of the joy of crying is looking at yourself looking incredibly sad and beautiful, instead I sacrificed another 20 minutes to dabbing away the streaks with yet more concealer and powder.

Then it was time to go outside . . .

ACNE: Time for action! Today's top-secret mission is going out and pretending everything is fine. Confidence is key!

During the day, I was obsessed with keeping my face clean, I'd make at least three trips to the toilet every lesson just to top up my foundation. Helpful souls would say things to me like, 'Try drinking more water, it'll really help,' or, 'You just need to clean your face properly.' Which I'd obviously never tried before, drinking only wine (am) and Monster Energy (pm), and washing only once a year when the stench became too overwhelming.

Even worse were the people who told me about bizarre things they'd read online, like, 'Oh my God I saw this article about how not washing your face clears up acne' (completely contradicting their earlier comments) or 'I heard soaking your face in your own urine is supposed to work wonders.' There was no way in hell I was going to skip washing my face, especially if I had to soak it in urine.

ACNE: OK, cadet. It's time to ramp things up.
Are you ready to feel some pain?

This is the thing about acne: it isn't just something you constantly notice on your face; it's also like someone's filled your face with tiny sharp rocks that are constantly being pressed like buttons. I would spend most days in constant agony, unable to think about anything else. Sometimes my cheeks and jawline would be in so much pain, I'd have to wash off and re-apply my make-up three or four times a day. I would, of course, add to the pain by picking and squeezing at them, wincing each time I burst a bulging whitehead and watched it splat comically onto the mirror. I'd grimace as I covered up the crime scene with yet more foundation.

ACNE: Lads, we're under attack. Spread out!
Multiply! Don't leave a patch uncovered!

Of course, nothing worked. I would go on nights out weighed down by the thought that my acne was a physical manifestation of my unattractiveness, my unworthiness. Pretty girls never seemed to have acne. There was no 'real skin' movement when I was at school. Every inch of bare skin on screen or in magazines had been airbrushed to within an inch of its life, first by make-up, then by computers.

I could barely afford to go out anyway, because I'd spent all my money on 'miracle products' recommended to me first by dermatologists, and then also by (acne-free) friends, strangers' blogs and even my grandmother. I would have sold my soul to the devil if the option was available, but I guess she was too busy giving world leaders terrible personalities and anxieties to a 17-year-old who just wanted to hit the clubs without feeling like Quasimodo.

Night after night, I would dab my skin with honey, toothpaste, witch hazel, tea tree or coconut oil, concocting a magic spell from a witches' handbook, wishing that tomorrow would be the day I woke up with beautiful, clear skin, Either that or I'd just accidentally created a health-enthusiast's edible treat on my chin.

> ACNE: This is a chemical weapons attack! Get huge, stay under the skin, do not let yourself be forced out! Try to intimidate the enemy with your size! They will never defeat us!

I was put on the contraceptive pill, which helped a bit, but the side-effects were terrible. I grew a thick coat of downy hair, giant fangs, my eyes turned red and I had a thirst for blood. I genuinely think if that was true, men would still be like, 'Well, at least I don't have to wear a condom, it just doesn't feel the same.' In actual fact, the pill just made me incredibly nauseous at night, which seems counterintuitive to its purpose. In fact, the first time I ever stayed over at a guy's house when I was 17, I needed to be sick so badly that I completely panicked and went and did it on the street outside his front door, only for his mum to return home and catch me in the act. We were both surprised: her, that a teenager was vomiting outside her door rather than in the perfectly good and available toilet, and me that it was actually only 8pm.

When I came off the pill, I made peace with the idea that I would just have to wear *Drag Race* levels of make-up every day for the rest of my life. I would have to make sure I never, ever sweated, even when exercising. When I slept over at a guy's house, I'd get up an hour before him to silently wash my face and do my make-up, before slipping back into bed and pretending I'd just woken up with flawless mascara and a contoured nose.

I think I mentioned that I worked on a banana farm in Australia, which isn't a euphemism, unless we're using it as code for 'working at an actual banana farm'. It was physical, monotonous work, in a frighteningly hot climate, which made wearing make-up almost impossible unless you were OK with it being halfway down your face by the end of the day.

ACNE: Stand down. We're no longer under threat. Remain medium-sized and ready for any sudden changes.

I stopped caring how my skin looked. I felt great. I felt

empowered. Sure I still had quote unquote 'bad skin', but who gave a fuck? I certainly didn't notice it as much, until one day at the hostel when I overheard two mean girls referring to me as 'that spotty bitch'. All because I got to ride a tractor at work that day. Honestly, banana farm politics are out of control.

All my insecurities came flooding back as I ran to my room and caked myself in an inch of concealer. A few days later, another girl in the hostel wanted to do a group photoshoot and asked that we all go bare-faced for it, but said to me, 'Can you apply concealer to hide your bad skin? I wouldn't want your spots to stand out.'

ACNE: Pizza face! Spotty bitch! Almond Magnum! Ha! You are a monster! You deserve nothing.

All day long my acne shouted these things to me, wearing me down, reminding me of my flaws, my weaknesses. I was defeated. I constantly craved Magnums but, mainly, I was sad.

Your skin is not your worth. In hindsight, I know that people don't get acne because they've done anything wrong, except for maybe putting toothpaste on their spots every night (please don't do this, it doesn't work and drying them out is not the best idea). If we got spotty toes, we'd put socks on and get on with our day, but because it often manifests on our face, we are tricked into thinking it is far more important than it is. It's like wearing a mask at

Halloween; it turns us into someone we're not, but it's just make-believe. You are not a cat. You are not Mike Myers. You are not a witch. You are *not* your acne.

I wish I could tell you I found a miracle cure, because I desperately searched for one for so many years, but I didn't. Acne is mostly hormonal, and that means there are lots of complex environmental factors that contribute to it, including some that doctors don't even fully understand. For me, my acne began to calm down when I changed a few things. I stopped crying all the time and focused on de-stressing and becoming a happier person. I quit coffee (that shit did my cortisol levels dirty). I embraced the banana farm and ignored the mean girls, who were also insecure about their flaws. I felt sorry for them too, because ultimately acne heals, but being a mean girl is forever (sometimes).

ACNE: Wait, are we . . . pacifists now?

I tried to wear my acne with pride so it didn't need to cause angry flare-ups for attention. I stopped using 'no more acne' as my birthday wish or writing it in my manifestation journal. I sorted out my gut, and focused on developing a diet that nourished me, but that also included Almond Magnums. I'd never tell anyone what to eat, but it really did help me to increase my consumption of whole foods and reduce my sugar intake a little. None of it was drastic, just minor changes. I stuck to a simple night-time and morning skincare routine, and stopped experimenting with new products every other month. I learned about what my skin really needed and what products were just there to zap you of all your money. I tried to make my skin feel safe and secure, and in doing so, I made myself feel safer and more secure as well.

ACNE: Retreat!

I also stopped using loads of dry shampoo and switched to natural deodorant. I don't know if this is science, but I worried that by plugging up some of the pores on my head and pits, everything was flooding out through my face like toxic goo in an alien movie. Anyway, it seemed to work. Of course, I still get spots, usually at the worst possible moment.

ACNE: Attention! Hayley's going on a date! Let's see what this guy's really made of . . . with a cluster of chin pimples.

But no one ever cares, and neither do I.

FOREHEAD: Hayley, I don't want to worry you but, what's that?

Since turning 30, I've got something new to obsess about: wrinkles. My forehead is criss-crossed with little lines, getting slightly deeper every day. When I look at them I think about the Grand Canyon, the Mariana Trench – you know, the deepest, darkest places on earth.

FOREHEAD: Can anyone hear an echo?

A crumbling noise, as the lines get even deeper
Staring at theses cavernous crevasses in the mirror
recently, I realised . . .

BRAIN: What the hell are you doing? Seriously,
what is this?

I'm looking at all my lines and thinking about how fine
they are. Well, not *fine*, but you know what I mean.

BRAIN: Look, I'm not here to say you look good,
but whack on some moisturiser and buck up your
ideas, we've got other stuff to think about. Like,
what job are we going to do? Are we all doomed
because of global warming? Will we ever find out
the meaning of life? Do we wipe our butt weird?

Brain is right. After worrying about my acne for so many
years, now when I catch myself staring into the mirror
at my lines and thinking the same thoughts, I know how
to redirect my attention. What are wrinkles anyway, but
a sign that you're getting older? I'm excited to get older!
Frankly, I can't wait to be 90 years old, sitting on a porch,
smoking a pipe, stroking my long grey beard and thinking, 'Ahh, what I'd do for a little bit of acne.'

Me vs Hormones

I was pretty shocked when I finally 'became a woman'. I thought it would be all high heels and red lipstick – sorry, I was a sexist child (I grew up in the 90s) – but I quickly realised it's mostly about learning to live with your violently fluctuating hormones, and fluctuating they are.

In my early teenage years, I'd gone from the girl who shaved the middle of her eyebrows to avoid the dreaded monobrow, to someone who also shaved all the way around them. By 16 I had two rather aggressive-looking Nike ticks on my forehead, reminding me to Just Do It, by which I mean grow my eyebrows back (they never did). Beyond the brows, I also had to shave my toes, pluck my nipple hairs, and address the fact that my butthole now wore a small wig. I understood that this was thanks to hormones, and it didn't bother me too much.

When it comes to gender dynamics in general, puberty isn't even so bad – people with uteruses get their periods for the first time, sure, but penis-owners can be just as spotty, hairy, awkward, smelly and self-conscious, plus they have the added issue of having to conceal involuntary boners every five minutes. It's adulthood that I want to raise a complaint about. I very much thought the deal with puberty was that it would one day be over, my hormones and I would make peace and I'd live a happy, joyful existence. Sadly, that hasn't been the case at all.

The first sign that my hormones and I were not going to become friends in adulthood was the violent reaction I started to develop to the phrase, 'Are you on your period?' I hate this question. It's never meant in the spirit of genuine inquiry, but always delivered with a slight sneer, as if to suggest that the only reason I might be feeling grumpy, annoyed or out of sorts is because I'm completely at the whim of my own bodily functions. Which I am but, like, shut up. Periods are horrible. They should make you mad. For three to five days every single month your uterus lining tears away, your back hurts, you can't get comfortable and you're absolutely exhausted. In a just world, we'd all get a paid week off work, plus a big round of applause as we left the office. We wouldn't pay for period products, and everyone would wait on us hand and foot.

The period itself is one thing, but in my opinion, the other stuff is even worse. It's like living in a horror film. One random, sunny day, I'll be minding my own business when, out of the corner of my eye, I notice that a tin of chickpeas is in the wrong location in the kitchen. Instantly, this is the single most upsetting thing I've ever experienced. I become convinced that my boyfriend has placed it there as a secret sign that he hates me, like some underground boyfriend illuminati stuff that I don't know about because I'm not on Reddit. How do I address this devastating chickpea situation? I begin to violently sob at the Lloyds TSB bank commercial, where black horses run wild in what can only be described as a very bleak-looking park in Wigan. Excuse me, am I being unreasonable?

BRAIN: No! You're completely right! Everything is terrible, we should definitely be lashing out.

It's not just crying either, although there's a lot of that. Over the next week, my reflection in the mirror changes and warps. I loathe the person staring back at me, and I assume that everyone else must loathe her too. My wardrobe becomes my worst enemy, as I can't imagine being someone who would wear anything I own. My jeans don't fit, my jumpers itch, in fact all my clothes are impossibly uncomfortable. All I want to do is eat, but when I do, I'm furious about it.

BRAIN: You're so gross. I can't believe you're still hungry.

I open another share-bag of popcorn.

BRAIN: You're pathetic. Look at you, eating. AGAIN.

I erupt into a flurry of tears. She's right. I'm disgusting, I hate myself. How dare I enjoy any piece of food in my time of despair?

Then it dawns on me. Aha! This must be the work of the moon. We must be coming up to a full moon. It really is the only possible explanation. I check on Google – yes! It's 13 days until the New Moon, which means the moon currently looks like one-third of a Jaffa Cake. Plus Mercury is in retrograde, I think. I have no idea what that means, but I want to blame something, so it might as well be Space. It's just like those planets to fuck with me.

I slump back on my sofa and pick up my phone, ready to delete my Instagram, break up with my boyfriend, and text, 'Why do you hate me?' to all my friends, because the moon told me to. That's when I spot it – my period tracking app. It's staring me straight in the face, practically winking at me. I open it and read the words: 'Period due in the next 4 days.' Fuck.

I didn't really know anything about how my period worked until I did my own research. It turns out my hormones have always been pretty imbalanced. I had hormonal acne until my mid-20s, and by 29 I was experiencing the worst PMS I had ever known, but I really didn't understand the extent of it. I figured that once a month, Period just knocked on the door of Hotel Vagina, asked for a room, treated the place like she was a noughties' rockstar and left five days later. Now I know it goes a little more like this . . .

A week or two before her trip, Period sends out a series of messages to the body, instructing everyone to look out for her arrival. It's the opposite of a baby shower – we're not getting ready to invite a new life into the world, we're prepping to take out the trash. There's a note for Stomach, telling her to appear more bloated, be an endless pit, and crave things she would have wanted during pregnancy . . . after all, it's her last chance for that. There's one for Boobs, telling them to swell up and get sore, and there's one for Face, instructing her to push pimples to the surface and become redder than ever. The last one is for Brain, telling her to carry on as normal, but she can't, because everything else is going haywire. She's the manager and this place is a mess.

Overwhelmed with complaints, Brain is excited for an excuse to be a full-on menace. She doesn't want to behave like a normal functioning brain, she wants destruction. Think it's OK to whistle a happy little song in the morning? How about a punch in the gut for you. Want to try and write a lovely poem? You're a piece of time-wasting shit who has never used a word correctly in her life. Want to do nothing? Well, that's not helping either, you lazy bitch! How dare you sit and relax? Soon, Brain is utterly exhausted. She's run out of engine power.

BRAIN: We should just die.

For once, I agree with her. We should just die.

BRAIN: Exactly, we're worthless and pointless
and every single person we know hates us.

Then, it's time. I'm woken abruptly by my body's alarm
clock at 7am on the dot, as the entire contents of my
arse need to evacuate my body to make room. It's never
ending. A gaggle of beavers arrives at my door as they've
heard there's a dam in my toilet that they want to nest in.
Right on cue, Period arrives. She's here with her suitcase
filled with back pain, breakdowns and cramps, ready to
settle in to the holiday from hell. Does she just stay in
her room? No way. Sometimes she'll pop out for the day
without telling me where she's going, only to get back in
the middle of the night and ruin a perfectly good pair
of pants.

On day five, I've had enough. Brain is sick of Period's
shit, too. Whether she's in or out, I refuse to use any form
of period product. She needs to know she's outstaying
her welcome. I will not be tending to her every need
anymore.

At last, she leaves, and we all breathe a sigh of relief.
Everything is fine. No, not fine, brilliant. I'm not disgusting! I'm not a terrible friend! My clothes are OK and my
personality is . . . also OK!

BRAIN: Let's not go crazy here.

The next three weeks pass, and I feel normal. I enjoy
my week of extroversion, where I want to be out and

socialising, and the world is a happy place to be. I start to forget about Period's stay and all the chaos she caused. I get my house in order. Perhaps next time it'll be different. I look out of the window at the bright, warm sun and think to myself—

BRAIN: Hang on, are those chickpeas out of place?

Brain vs Ballistic Missile

It's my birthday tomorrow, and I'm still pinching myself that I'm spending it in Hawaii. I've never really loved celebrating my birthday, but I've always loved the fact that it's the one time of the year when you can shamelessly get out of anything all month long. Don't fancy going to a work event? Sorry, I can't come, it's my birthday. Debating who's going to cook dinner tonight? Can't be me, it's my birthday month. Works like a charm every time.

From 1st January to 1st February (my birthday is all month long) I treat myself constantly. A new top? Why not! Branded mayonnaise instead of supermarket own? Yes please! An excuse to get out of literally anything I don't want to do? I'll take ten! But visiting Hawaii? This is seriously a dream come true. I spent every single penny in my savings account and worked two jobs for six days a week to make it happen. Even though I'll probably be living off cups of noodles for the rest of my life, it'll be worth it. I'm used to spending my winter birthday shivering, but this year I'm planning to spend the day lounging on the beach.

My boyfriend Simon and I arrived late last night, which means I haven't had a chance to look around yet. All I've seen is the inside of this hotel room, which is already amazing. The bed is huge and the bathroom smells like piña coladas. Thanks to jet-lag I've been awake since 4am, and I've spent that time watching the sun rise through the massive window over the Hawaiian shore. It's gorgeous. I already feel relaxed, like the rest of the world has melted away. I even think about turning off my phone.

> BRAIN: Let's not go crazy. You've still got to take photos.

Brain is right; I can't just not take photos. I'll probably never come back here ever again. I do a huge yawn, like a girl in a bed advert, and head to the bathroom, where I balance my phone on the side of the sink. It's almost time for breakfast and I'm starving, but I can hear Simon on the balcony video-calling his family. As soon as he's done, I'm ready to hit the breakfast buffet to fuel up for a long, luxurious day of nothing. I plonk myself on the toilet.

Out of nowhere, a siren starts blaring from my phone. It's loud. Like, really loud. I wonder why I would have set an alarm to go off at 8.07am, and why I chose such a horrible noise versus my usual completely ineffective tinkling of bells. What a fool, I chuckle to myself, before reaching for my phone. On the screen I read: BAL-LISTIC MISSILE THREAT INBOUND TO HAWAII. SEEK IMMEDIATE SHELTER. THIS IS NOT A DRILL.

Have you ever thought about where you'll be when you find out exactly how you're going to die? Perhaps on a sinking cruise ship, on a plane that's plunging to the ground, or in the jaws of a giant reanimated dinosaur. Me, I was mid-poop.

BRAIN: Well, shit. I mean, at least it's on brand.

The first thought that pops into my head is that I probably won't be leaving this hotel room today.

BRAIN: Yeah, and you know what sucks even more? In a few short minutes, we're going to be dead.

Actually . . . is it a few minutes? I've been standing frozen in the bathroom with my pants around my ankles, so I have no idea how much time has already passed. The feeling is like when you hear a fire alarm at work, and you can't quite decide how much you're supposed to panic. Get up and run from the building screaming and it turns out to be a drill? You've humiliated yourself so badly you'll have to quit your job. Stay at your desk to finish up the spreadsheet and it's real? You're burning to death, which is also incredibly embarrassing. Can you imagine everyone at your funeral? Someone will say, 'At least she died doing what she loved: finishing the spreadsheets,' while they're all secretly promising themselves they'll never be as much of a loser as you.

Simon saunters in. He's also heard the alarm and seen the message, but we're both acting like it's a completely normal thing to have learned you're about to die. He's decided that in light of the recent news, he really needs to brush his teeth. That's right, if he's being evaporated, he's doing it with minty fresh breath. I stand and watch him in complete silence as he brushes, flosses and swishes with mouthwash. His dental hygiene is impeccable.

BRAIN: This really isn't the time. Didn't the alert say to seek immediate shelter?

It did! I look around the room and assess our options. There's a table, but it's pretty flimsy. We could both get inside the wardrobe, but the doors are a bit wobbly so I don't really see how that would help. What is the protocol for escaping a missile? We could lie on the bed like that old couple in *Titanic*, only we've not been together *that* long. It feels a bit too intimate. I wonder who will play me in the movie of the Ballistic Missile. Perhaps Margot Robbie. Oh, or Anya Taylor-Joy . . .

BRAIN: Hayley, please, concentrate.

Oh yeah, shelter. Simon and I put on our flip-flops and leave the room, flipping and flopping along the corridor towards the lift. You can see the pool from one of the windows in the hallway. It's kind of eerie, like something you'd see in a disaster movie. All the rubber dinghies have been abandoned and towels, flip-flops and sunglasses just left where they are as everyone dashed away.

When we get to the lift, we bump into a family made up of an ex-military dad, an incredibly strong-looking woman, who I presume is the mum, and four kids. He's barking orders at them, and we instinctively fall into line. He seems like he knows what he's doing and as we don't, it's obvious we need to follow. He shouts, 'This is not a drill!'

It actually hadn't occurred to me that it could possibly be a drill. The lift doors open, but it's already packed with people. Lots of stressed, crying people. Army Dad starts herding us all towards the stairs. The stairwell is flooded with shouting kids and screaming parents, all jostling to get out.

BRAIN: Imagine if you tripped down the stairs right now, how embarrassing would that be?

For the first time in my life – faced with my imminent death – I don't let Brain's promise of very minor embarrassment throw me off my mission, which is to . . . uh, actually, I have no idea what I'm doing. I just keep running. Ten storeys is a lot and I'm completely out of breath by the time Simon and I burst through the exit door.

Swept up by the crowd, we start to head along the street away from the hotel. I pull out my phone and call my mum. It rings six times, before she picks up and says, 'I'm just heading into Zumba, can we talk later?'

I don't know if you've ever had to delay your mum's entry into Zumba class to tell her the news that you're about to be blown into a thousand pieces by a ballistic missile, but, to her credit, she stayed incredibly calm. She was confused, of course, and I'm not sure she really believed me for the first few seconds, but she made me promise to keep her updated, then – and I'll never, ever be able to verify this – I'm 90 per cent sure she headed into Zumba anyway.

Meanwhile, people on the street had begun telling us to turn around and head back to the hotel. Simon pulled up an article on his phone called 'How To Survive A Nuclear Explosion', which we concluded was probably about the same as a ballistic missile. The main suggestion was to go to the basement or the middle of a building and stay very, very clear of the outside world.

BRAIN: I knew we should have got into the wardrobe.

There's no way I'm climbing back up ten flights of stairs. I'd rather die.

By the time we get back to the hotel, it becomes devastatingly obvious that this is not a structure designed to protect you from the outside world. If anything, it's the opposite. It's got a real outside/inside thing going on. Great light, I think, as I slump against the base of a lobby armchair. Alongside dozens of other visitors, we sit on the lobby floor and wait for the end.

You'd hope that the final moments before death would be a time to reflect on the full and fascinating life you've lived, but my mind has gone completely blank. The room is oddly quiet, no one's really looking at anyone else. I think about saying something, but there's no small talk that really cuts through the knowledge you're about to not exist.

BRAIN: Is this supposed to feel so awkward?

A weird thing to think in the pregnant silence of death, but I'm not great at silence at the best of times. If I'm speaking to someone at a party and they pause to breathe, I immediately have to say something completely unrelated to the conversation, like, 'Aren't those curtains thick?' or, 'Does bread sometimes make anyone else's tummy hurt?' Sitting in a lobby full of strangers waiting to evaporate into nothingness? This is my hell, and not even for the reason you'd expect.

BRAIN: Seriously, this is agony. It feels like time is going so slowly. How long have we been here?

How long *have* we been here? I look at my phone. It's been way over half an hour since the alert. How long do ballistic missiles take? I think about asking Simon to look at the article again, but then I notice that he's playing a game on his phone and decide not to disturb his peace. I close my eyes, sit back and wait for death.

Suddenly, everyone's phones start beeping simultaneously. A new message has arrived. Everyone jumps a little, preparing for another terrible display: THERE IS NO MISSILE THREAT OR DANGER TO THE STATE OF HAWAII. REPEAT. FALSE ALARM.

The government later claim it was a mistake. I'm not sure if someone can really just slip onto a control board in a high-security room and accidentally type out a terrifying and life-threatening message, but hey! At least I'm not dead.

I text my mum, and 15 minutes later she calls me back, suspiciously out of breath. I tell her I'm not going to die. That it was a mistake. She's cheery, 'Thank goodness for that! Very good news, now get out there and have the best day possible!'

It is good news. Simon and I stand up and head to the breakfast buffet.

Brain vs Gut

I've woken up with a knot in my belly that I can't seem to shake. It's an uneasy sensation, not quite physical but not entirely mental either. My stomach is churning, my knees feel wobbly and my gut is gurgling like it's sending me a message. Gut has always been a little bit psychic, so I try to tune in and listen, though she's usually only right about 98 per cent of the time. It's a bit of a two truths one lie situation. Usually she'll wake me up and say something like . . .

GUT: I see rain, a proposal from a dear friend and I predict a dog will hump your leg.

It's always fairly easy to sift the truths from the lie. It's the middle of the summer and we're in a drought, so I know I'll have my leg dry humped and probably be invited to the cinema – it's not exactly a proposal, but Gut does like to speak in riddles.

This morning, she seems very confident. Maybe too confident.

GUT: Ahhhh, my child, I see uncertainty in your future. Also, breakfast.

I eat some toast, but the feeling doesn't go away.

GUT: Oh, and your boyfriend is cheating on you.

Wait, what? No two truths and a lie today, just a rather aggressive statement. As strange as it is to hear Gut say this seemingly out of the blue, something about it immediately feels true. I'm currently in a long-distance relationship with Simon. We've gone our whole relationship living together but now because of work opportunities he's living and working in Oxford while I've just started a new job in Brighton. It's only a two-hour drive, but it feels worlds away. Having been so used to living in the same flat as him for so long, it feels hard. I'm lonely.

Most of the time we talk back and forth on Facebook Messenger. I have no idea why we choose that particular platform for our messaging. It's easy to fall into grooves at the start of a relationship: some people speak to each other in baby voices, others slag each other off to mutual friends, but Simon and I like to chat on the platform used exclusively by kooky aunts and incels. On Messenger, I can not only see if he's read my last message, but also if he is or has recently been online. You'd think this would be reassuring, but it's making me crazy.

Today, I can see that he's been online, but for some reason he's left my message unread. I watch him come online, and then go off again. My message remains unopened. What the hell?

GUT: He's avoiding you.

I've always been terrified of being a 'psycho' girlfriend. Pop culture tells us that's the worst type of woman we can possibly be – overbearing, controlling, manipulative – and I take this kind of thing very seriously. I shrug off Gut's words. Simon's not avoiding me. He's my boyfriend and he loves me. He's just busy, he's probably popped online to chat with his mum or nan. No one else uses Facebook anyway. Still, I've just started this new job and I can barely concentrate at work because I'm so anxious about it. And even if he isn't cheating on me, this feeling can't be right . . . Can it?

BRAIN: Love is pain. If you're not feeling
anxious, it's not real love, everybody knows that.

A week later and I'm acting without any rationality. The stress of remaining easy and breezy in front of my boyfriend while also analysing his every move for clues that he has, at best, gone off me, or, at worst, is cheating on me, has become almost overwhelming. I'm not eating, not sleeping, and I'm barely getting any work done. This is always my vibe in an office, but it's so bad that I'm not even trying to cover my tracks. I spend all day, every day, staring at my phone. Simon's still not really replying to my messages, and when we do talk he seems distant, like he's not very interested in me. People at work are starting to notice how little I'm getting done, but I don't give a shit. I'm far too concerned about Simon.

BRAIN: Maybe you should say something more interesting. Oooh, I know! Tell him you found a dead body in the stationery cupboard!

This would check out, because I've practically become a professional Agatha Christie impersonator, paying closer attention to Simon than ever before. When I'm not watching to see if he's on Facebook Messenger, I'm looking through his Instagram to see who he's been inter-acting with. Gut watches as I scroll:

GUT: I see . . . a famous model.

I see her too, but I'm not worried. Let's be honest, she's way out of any regular human being's league and her inbox is probably overflowing with messages. She'd never spot his.

GUT: I see . . . a friend of his from university.

I've met this friend too, and I'm pretty sure there's noth-ing going on between them. Plus, she has a really fit boy-friend and seems like a very genuine person.

GUT: I see . . . his co-worker.

Ah, yes. This one makes me feel weird. I can see on his feed that they've been liking each other's photos religiously, sometimes even commenting cute things underneath, and that's just what I can see. Who knows what they're saying to each other in private? Oh God, my stomach is churning again.

GUT: Find out.

What, guess his password? No, I can't do that.

BRAIN: Do it.

Well, two against one, I suppose. I log out of my Instagram and open the Sign In page in incognito mode. My heart is thumping in my chest. It doesn't matter, I think, because I won't be able to guess his password anyway.

BRAIN: Try his cat's name.

GUT: I agree. He probably is the kind of person to have an obvious password. I predict it'll be his cat's name, too.

Don't be ridiculous. I type it in and . . . *bingo*. Thanks, Ralph. You're a good boy.

My hands are shaking with the adrenaline. I didn't think I'd be able to guess his password so easily. I open his direct messages and scroll through, looking for any names

I recognise, but there's nothing. There are no messages from any girls. Not even female friends. This is actually a bit weird. Why doesn't he have any female friends?

What am I saying? This is good news. I should be jumping for joy.

GUT: I don't know, something still doesn't feel right.

Oh, come on! We checked! I message to tell him I love him. Four hours later, he sends back a single 'x'. Right, that's odd. What happened to the long love messages he used to send me?

A couple of weeks pass, during which I've been resisting the urge to check his messages again, and I find myself home alone on a Friday night. I'd suggested to Simon that we meet up, but he said he was finishing late and was then going to head out with the guys from rugby to celebrate the end of the work week, so we don't. When we first moved apart we used to message right up until bedtime, but these days I barely hear from him after midday. I've brought this up in a few phone calls, but he brushes it off like I'm being needy.

BRAIN: You are pretty needy. Remember when you kept demanding that your parents wipe your arse all the time?

I was a baby! I didn't know how to wipe my arse. But I'm not a baby now. I'm an adult with a boyfriend who only very occasionally messages me, and surely I should be getting more attention than this.

BRAIN: Message him to see how his night is going.

I send him a quick 'how's things?' and, once again, it's left unread. I can see him coming on and off Messenger, but he's not replying to me. The familiar stomach knot is back. I try to get ready to go out, but I can't think about anything else. This is ruining my evening. I should be leaving to go out with friends now, but I'm so late, I might as well just stay home.

BRAIN: Check his Facebook Messenger.

No, I can't invade his privacy again.

GUT: To know the truth, you must look inside.

. . . myself?

GUT: Sorry, no. Inside his messages. Seriously,
Brain is right, you should do it, see what he's hiding.

Fine. I did it once, what's one more peek? I grab my laptop and open incognito mode.

BRAIN: *Dum dum dum dum, dum dum dum dum*

Sorry, are you saying I'm dumb?

> BRAIN: The opposite! I'm doing the Mission
> Impossible theme tune. Plus, you're making a great
> decision. I can't wait to randomly remind you
> about this in the future while you're trying to get
> to sleep. It'll really keep you up at night thinking
> about how you invaded your beloved boyfriend's
> privacy and broke a bond of trust.

I certainly am breaking a bond of trust, but at this point
I cannot help myself. I cautiously type his credentials
and I'm in. This time I'm even more nervous than before.
I pace around the room, trying to decide if I should actually do it. There's no way he's cheating on me. He's just
a busy person enjoying a night out with his work friends
and I'm a little hacker rat. It's me who's the villain. Plus,
we've had so many good times together. Things are actually going really well, I think.

> BRAIN: Going well? He doesn't even talk to us
> anymore. You're basically single at this point.

That's not true, we're just comfortable with not talking
to each other. This is real love.

> GUT: Forget your past and face your future.

I look down.

It's bad. Gut was right. He's been seeing this girl he works with.

I read everything. They talk constantly – day and night, from morning until bedtime. They meet up regularly outside of work. They've discussed keeping it a secret from me. My heart feels like it's going to fall out of my arse. I run to the toilet and I'm sure my body is rejecting him; it's the only way I can explain the bowel evacuation I just went through.

I message Simon that we're breaking up. He replies immediately.

I don't. I delete and block him off every social media platform.

Straight away, Gut feels better. I'm sad, of course, but after so much tension, it's a huge relief to know the truth.

When it comes to Gut and love, she seems to always just know. I will never understand how she plucked that particular feeling out of thin air, when there was no real rhyme or reason to suggest anything was going on before I started probing. I had desperately wanted her to be wrong. I wanted her to be like, 'Hah! Prank! Gotcha! He's not cheating after all, but your hamster? He's going to die in seven days.' Instead, I'm left feeling like a complete lemon, wondering how many people knew he was cheating on me and why he was more comfortable staying in a relationship he knew wasn't making him happy than just breaking up with me.

There's a lot of things that suck about being cheated on, but mainly I tried to figure out what it was about me that wasn't good enough. Did I talk about poop too much? Was I too needy? Not needy enough? Was it because I won't have anal sex or that I fart uncontrollably in my sleep?

BRAIN: What about 'all of the above'?

Thankfully, I think it's probably nothing to do with me as a person or the fact I won't have anal sex. It's normally something to do with the other person and what they want out of life, and they more than likely didn't do it to hurt you on purpose. I'm just grateful Gut opened my eyes to it before it went on any longer.

I think women are often drawn to spiritual things like astrology for this very reason. The truth can be so relative, so ephemerous, so hard to pin down, that we seek out things that help us make sense of our world when the truth seems out of reach. I've never been a particularly mystic person but since the old hacker debacle I am trying to listen to Gut more.

The only time I've ever been fully swayed by mysticism was in Australia, on the banana farm. As you can probably imagine, my banana farm era was not one full of intentional choices, so even though it was a lot of fun, I was feeling pretty lost. One evening, for a laugh, a couple of the girls suggested we go to Mission Beach to see a psychic and it was cheap enough that I agreed. The tarot reader pulled out a few cards and told me that I was a beautiful person, warm and full of sunshine. What a great grift, I thought, just tell people exactly what they want to hear.

Then, out of nowhere, she shouted, 'Baby girl!'

I was stunned. I looked down at my stomach and she nodded, 'Yes. It's a girl.'

BRAIN: She's making a comment about our weight.

It's no secret that during my farming days I put on a stone or two. There's not an awful lot else to do when you're working on a farm apart from eat and drink beer. But there certainly wasn't a baby in my tummy. Though I am often convinced I'm pregnant, I knew for a fact that in that moment I was not, unless it was an immaculate conception, which I highly doubted. I realised she might just be a bit of a phony.

Then she paused. She told me she could see my dad standing behind my left shoulder with his back to me, and my mum running frantically back and forth in front of me. This was a strange turn in what I had assumed would just be a run of endless compliments and random stabs in the dark. Plus, it didn't make any sense – my mum was a pretty chill person, and my dad was my best friend. He would never turn away from me. Ridiculous.

As I left the psychic, that familiar sensation from Gut was there.

GUT: Something's wrong. You should ask Mum about it.

Honestly, I couldn't imagine anything weirder than calling my mum at 7am to ask her if she'd been frantically running about, but I had promised to listen more to Gut, and Brain seemed to agree.

BRAIN: Yup, Gut's right. We should ask her.

I took out my phone and called my mum. Looking out to sea, I told her what the psychic had said about Dad turning away from me, and her running frantically back and forth. I was expecting her to laugh, to tell me it was ridiculous, barbaric in fact – she'd say, 'Go and ask for a refund!', but instead she took a long, deep breath before replying, 'Hayley, your dad is ill.'

She explained that she thought my dad may have a brain tumour. He'd been acting strangely. His personality had changed. He seemed different. Cold. I'd never heard her sound so serious. My mum was panicking because she'd decided to sell the house and downsize because my dad was no longer working, but she was worried: 'How do I know if I'm making the right decision?'

I listened to my Gut.

GUT: It's time to go home.

Dad vs Brain

Five months after I left Australia, I found myself in Orlando, Florida, working at Disney World. This had always been part of the plan. I left Australia early and returned home for a month before my US visa started. I really didn't want to leave my family, but my mum kept insisting that I couldn't put my life on hold. She'd say, 'Whatever happens to your dad, he'll still be here in a year. He'd be devastated to know you didn't take a job you'd been so excited for because he wasn't well.'

It felt wrong. So wrong. Like I was ditching my family out of selfishness, but we still had no idea what was going on with my dad and she told me there was nothing I could do to help, so reluctantly I left.

Now it's four days until Christmas Day and I feel like I'm living inside a bubble of false reality. My life at Disney is about making guests feel special. I make 'magic' for people from all over the world . . . by pouring them beers. Last night I finished a late shift and I'm still in bed at 2pm. I don't have work today until 4pm, so I can stay where I am until then. My mum should be calling any minute to let me know the results of my dad's CT scan and other tests. She hasn't told me an awful lot about what's been going on recently, and I suspect it's because she's trying to protect me. But at 23 years old, I don't feel she needs to.

In my own mind, I've decided it's the medication he's on. He's had cluster headaches for most of my life and has been on various pills, injections and strong pain-killers to try and treat them. They almost never work, but they do provide some light relief. They changed his dose earlier this year when things started to go downhill.

My phone buzzes into action. It's my mum.

GUT: Brace yourself.

I take a long breath in through my nose, and my shoulders rise up to my ears. Please, please, please don't be anything serious. Please say it's not a brain tumour. I answer. As soon as she speaks I can hear it in her voice. It's not steady and calm like usual. It's shaky and high. Something is really fucking wrong. I want to hurry her along to the diagnosis, but I know this must be as hard for her as it is for me. The tears are forming at the back of my eyes. It feels like hours before she comes out with it.

GUT: It's really bad. Really, really bad. Your life is about to change.

At last, Mum says as calmly as she can, 'I'm so sorry, Hayley, your dad has dementia.'

Of all the things in the world I expected to hear, this was the very last. At 60 years old, four days before Christmas and over 4,000 miles away from me, my dad has been diagnosed with Pick's disease. A rare form of very aggressive dementia.

BRAIN: Fuck.

I've got no idea how to respond to what my mum has just said to me. Dementia? My grandpa had Alzheimer's, but he got that in his 80s. This shouldn't be happening to a 60-year-old. How can I have a dad with dementia when I'm only 23? I don't understand. He's always been a constant in my life. He's always got all the answers. He's so smart. When my grandpa died, my dad did everything he could to prevent anything like that happening to him. He changed his diet and learned Spanish. He ensured he was always using his brain. He was incredibly healthy and switched on. He doesn't deserve this. He's always done everything for this family, he's put all of us before himself, through everything. He's had to suffer with cluster headaches for well over a decade. How on earth could life be this fucking cruel?

I tell my mum I'm booking a flight and coming home. I can't be in America when my family needs me. But she isn't having any of it. She's serious. She tells me, 'Don't you dare come home. Life is so precious, and you never know when it's going to be taken from you.'

So I stay.

It's hard. Really hard. I feel so much guilt. I call and text every day for updates. I want to make sure everyone is OK. My behaviour changes while I'm away. I'm less happy than I was before this news. I'm angry, I'm sad and I feel a heaviness in my body that makes waking up every day more difficult. I just want things to be the way they were. A few weeks before I'm due to come home, my mum warns me it's going to be a shock seeing my dad. I've had little to no contact with him while I've been away, because he has no attention span for speaking on the phone. It's been incredibly strange feeling so disconnected from someone I'm used to speaking to at least six times a day.

Finally, my contract ends and I fly home, but it's not the home I'm used to. My parents have sold the family house and moved to a new area, into a smaller place that's built for a couple. This new house is upside down – upstairs is downstairs and downstairs is upstairs, a nice little metaphor for how my life now feels. Walking through the front door is surreal. It's like I've walked into a stranger's life, rather than the one I've known and loved. It smells different. It looks different. It is different.

My mum envelops me in a big hug, and my brother and sister-in-law welcome me home with as much energy as they can muster. I notice that my dad isn't there to greet me. I ask where he is and we all go to find him.

As I walk down the stairs, he emerges from the master bedroom. The man I once knew better than anyone in the world looks like a completely different person. He's gaunt and grey. He always dyed his hair when he was well, but he's let it go. He looks confused, sad, like someone has sucked all the life out of him. I burst into tears and go over for a cuddle. He just laughs. I don't understand any of it. Why is he laughing? Who is this person?

Pick's disease is a cruel dementia. All dementia is cruel, but this one's especially bad. It strips a person of their personality, changes their behaviour and takes away control of their emotions. It reduces your life expectancy to seven years. In the end, you lose the ability to use language. In this moment, the guilt comes flooding in hard and fast. I feel like I have missed the last months of knowing my dad for who he was. I've ripped it from myself. I try to talk to him. I say I love him and missed him. He tells me, 'Everyone thinks I've got dementia, but I don't.'

I move back in with my mum and dad for the next nine months and try to help out as much as I can. It's hard, though. When you're confronted with someone with dementia, you're mourning the loss of them while they are still alive. The person you once knew is fading into the background while their shell stays in place. Their shell holds all of your memories, everything factual, while their personality is different in every way. They don't behave the way you are used to; they don't respond to the things you say in the way they once did. I feel as though I have been robbed. I feel helpless and angry and confused as to how it all happened so quickly. My mum, brother and

I live by the phrase, 'If you don't laugh, you'll cry.' We look for the humour in everything, and sometimes it isn't too hard.

At a birthday meal for my auntie, my dad is so desperate for his dinner that he gets up from the table, heads into the kitchen and demands to know where it is. We spend the rest of the meal with him trapped between my mum and brother so he can't dart back into the kitchen.

He's adopted lad culture. Every drink you pass him he downs in seconds. My brother and I have started chanting, 'See that drink away, see that drink away,' as he does it, just to keep all of our spirits up.

The morning he meets my new boyfriend – who I met while working at Disney for the first time – I've nipped out to the corner shop to grab some breakfast and left him in my bed. My dad comes into the room and pulls the duvet off him, revealing my half-naked, half-asleep boyfriend. He stares at him and says, 'Oh, I thought you were Ollie.'

Ollie is my brother, who most definitely wouldn't be asleep, undressed, in my bed. My dad extends his hand to shake my new boyfriend's, but keeps shaking, and shaking, and shaking. He won't let go until my brother comes in and intervenes. We laugh at that one for weeks. My boyfriend and I eventually break up, which comes as no surprise after that frankly jarring experience.

Over time, we start having to keep my dad locked in the house with us at night. He's becoming a masterful escape artist. A real Harry Houdini. We lock the front door and keep all the windows closed, but he's determined to get out. On one occasion, he tries to climb out of the downstairs window, but my brother catches him before he can swing his second leg over the frame. When he does manage to get out, he runs up to the leisure centre where my mum teaches aerobics and stands at the back of the class, waving at her.

One night I come home late from work and accidently leave the key in the front door. I'm asleep for an hour before I'm woken up by the slow turn of the key in the lock. I leap out of bed like a whippet on speed and catch my dad exiting the front door in just his pants. He makes a run for it. The two of us sprint down the road in the middle of the night, as passers-by from local pubs watch on in complete confusion. Thankfully, it isn't too long until I catch him and coax him back home and into bed.

Eventually, the doctor tells us it's no longer safe for Dad to be living at home with us. We knew this was coming. He needs round the clock supervision and we were struggling. My mum chooses a care home for him that is less than a mile from our house, so we can visit him as often as possible.

I'm not there the day he moves into full-time care, and it's a week later that I first go to the home to see him. My dad. My best friend. The strongest man I know. He looks weak, vulnerable and lost. It's one of the most harrowing moments of my life, that is burned into my memory. He doesn't seem like my dad anymore. The memories of my dad as I'd always known him start to fade away in my mind. The man that was my everything is being replaced by this new version of him. I find it so difficult to remember how he used to be. Past conversations, past experiences we've shared. That part of Brain seems to have been removed. Every visit feels like a piece of me is dying with him. It really hurts seeing him in there. Everyone looks so old in comparison to him, I can't get my head around it. We play basketball, catch and ping-pong every time I visit and he still beats me. His hand—eye coordination and knack for ball games never goes, and mine never improves. The one thing that keeps our spirits up is that he seems happier. His carers are like his buddies and they look after him so beautifully. I am so grateful to both of them.

The last time I was actually able to see my dad was before the pandemic. We lost two years of visits because of that virus. He was all alone in the care home with no idea what was going on or why we had abandoned him. When we are finally allowed in, they have him behind a metal fence. He sits opposite my brother and I on Father's Day as he eats his dinner and we hand him our cards and presents. I do everything I can not to cry.

Me vs Grief

You're not taught to grieve. I wish it was something we learned in school. It seems crazy that we don't take the time to cover how to handle one of the most transformational moments in life. Instead, we learn:

- Pythagoras theorem
- How to make paper people
- How to get battery power from a potato

That last one seems particularly pointless. When, in my time of need, would I possibly be required to stab a potato with wired rods to power a tiny clock?

On 13th April 2021, my dad died. I was utterly fucking broken by the news. Although he'd had dementia for the past five years, it still came as a shock. It had just been his 65th birthday; his card and present were still sat in my car. I was supposed to drop them over to my mum as she was the only one authorised to visit him at the care home during the final lockdown. I'd missed the window of getting them over to her because of work commitments. I felt the most immense guilt knowing he didn't get his birthday card and present from me. What if he'd thought I didn't love him anymore?

That morning, I woke up and felt a heaviness in my body. I was tired, really tired. I wasn't ready to leave my bed, so was scrolling through my phone when the call from my mum came through.

Her voice kept catching in her throat as she spoke, and she kept apologising. As the words left her mouth, I fell to the floor in complete agony. It was every bit as dramatic as it sounds. Still, the tears felt odd. They were already streaming as I tried to understand what she had just said to me. On the drive over to her house, I shed enough liquid to fill a beer keg. I got through half a toilet roll with the amount of slime pouring from my nose. Still, I didn't understand what was happening. I remember the events of that day moment by moment. I know the exact angle I was laying at when my phone rang and the thoughts that ran through my mind as my mum's number popped up on my phone. I have constant flashbacks of it. All of it.

It was still lockdown. My entire family had been so strict with the rules, but there we were, all in the same room together. We hugged, we cried and we didn't even crack a window. I know, we were hardcore. It felt so good to all be together, to reminisce on all the stories of my dad that we'd forgotten. I felt his absence so desperately, I would have done anything in that moment to take the last five years back. To have made some sort of change, to have done something to keep him here. I just wanted him to have had his whole life the way it should have been.

A few days after my dad passed away, I did a Google search for 'how to grieve'. I'd started to worry I was doing it wrong. This is when I came across an acrostic called SARAH, which is a model for how many people respond to grief:

S – SHOCK
A – ANGER
R – REJECTION
A – ACCEPTANCE
H – HEALING

It made a lot of sense, but it wasn't exactly how my journey felt. Mine was more like this:

H – HARDY
A – ANGER
Y – YAWNING
L – LAUGHTER
E – ENVY
Y – YES, OK, THIS HAS HAPPENED

Sorry, I'm rubbish at acrostics.

Hardy

After the initial tears, I decided my job was to be brave, strong, and there for the rest of the family. I took on a portion of the phone calls to family members, delivering that news over and over again. When you make those kinds of calls you have to re-live the devastation with every unsuspecting family member, pausing silently on the phone as they react to the news.

The day my dad died, I don't remember any of us crying for longer than a few hours. Straight away, we all pulled together. We told stories about him, enjoyed each other's company and tried to keep a sense of normality. The reality hadn't settled in, but we all wanted to support my mum. Nothing was ever going to compare to how my mum was feeling; I couldn't even imagine what receiving that news must have been like for her. I remember worrying that if ghosts existed and my dad was in the room that day, he might have thought we were all acting as if nothing had happened, or even that we were glad he was gone. Later on, I spoke to him as if he was in the room and told him we missed him, that we were all devastated, and that life would never be the same again – just to be sure.

As I tried to fall asleep that first night, I felt the most intense shooting pains in my chest.

DOCTOR BRAIN: We're dying from a heart attack.

I felt oddly calm about the possibility. The pain was intense and didn't feel as though it would relent. I wondered if this was what it was like to die of a broken heart.

257

For the first time in my life, I didn't feel scared at the thought of dying. Oddly, the idea of being reunited with my dad is the only thing that has ever really calmed my health anxiety.

The day of the funeral arrived and I spent the morning fussing over work. It was like I couldn't allow myself to focus on what was happening. If I let my thoughts drift, I'd get caught up in them and the heartbreak and all its pain would return. He wasn't supposed to be gone at 65. It felt absurd. There were so many more moments we were supposed to experience. He was meant to retire and enjoy years of happiness. None of it made sense to me.

Seeing the hearse arrive was chilling, but seeing his coffin knocked the wind out of me. It was only a short service, as crematoriums are a conveyor belt of funerals. Still, it was exactly how we wanted it to be. We had a celebrant who told the story of his life and we all laughed and cried along, remembering the hero that was my dad. We played his favourite songs and I read a eulogy. I was, of course, self-centred enough to feel nervous about public-speaking.

We held the wake in the garden of my parents' house. It was still lockdown and so we weren't allowed to have a large number of people in the house. It absolutely pissed it down, with sideways rain and strong gusts of wind. We all agreed it was probably dad's doing, it was exactly the type of humour he had. Still we raised a beer for him, and my family and I got to hear about him and some of his funniest moments through the words of his best mates and work colleagues. I had never felt more proud to be my dad's daughter.

Anger

This stage was arguably one of the worst. After the funeral, I turned into a very angry little lady indeed. It came out of nowhere. I've never considered myself to be an angry person, but I'd be curled up on the sofa watching a film when all of a sudden rage would pulse through my body. The next thing I knew, I'd be punching the shit out of my throw cushions. It was an incredibly odd experience, punching navy-blue velvet cushions for absolutely no reason. They were soft, plump and they had only ever supported me, but there I was wishing death upon them. My face would burn red, so I'd go outside in whatever I was wearing and run until the rage stopped. One day I left the house in a pair of Mickey Mouse pyjama bottoms and a vest top and just ran continuously down the road. Three cars honked their horn at me, which only unleashed more rage.

Yawning

I spent a lot of time after my dad died in bed or passed out on the sofa. I didn't really understand what was going on at the time, I just figured I was maybe dying too. I'd wake up in the morning and feel like I had been hit by a bus, then dragged along by a train, and eventually squashed between two massive walls.

A typical day would go something like this:

- Alarm at 7am
- Snooze alarm till 9.30am
- Get out of bed and go to the sofa with duvet
- Lay on the sofa, with a film playing in the background, and drink tea
- Pass out until midday
- Wake up and have breakfast
- Pass out until 3pm
- Wake up and watch something
- Make dinner
- Pass out till 7pm
- Go to bed

I could barely keep my eyes open. This stage went on for ages and felt like it was never going to end. When I'd see my family I'd try to be peppy, but the second I got home, regardless of the time, I'd get straight into bed and be in and out of sleep until morning. This entire phase is quite foggy to me, so much of this stage of my grief feels like a gap in my history. I think Brain was doing all she could to protect me.

Laughter

I would sometimes still imagine that my dad wasn't dead, that he was just down the road in the care home. None of it felt real. A week after his funeral, I chose to go and collect his ashes. It was part of my process. I figured if I went to get them myself, I'd be able to register what had happened.

As I stepped into the funeral home I was showered with attention. Everyone was patting me on the back and giving me their condolences. The people who work at funeral homes must be in a constant state of sympathy. I was waved through to the back room, where I was handed my dad's ashes in a fancy, bright white gift bag. It felt like I'd just purchased a designer item in a very expensive store. Remains: by Gucci.

As I took the bag from the funeral director, I commented on how heavy my dad still was.

> BRAIN: Oh my God! Did you just body-shame a dead person?

I rushed back to the car and drove home with my dead dad, now in his gift bag, strapped into the passenger seat. Once there, my mum and brother gathered around for the unpacking. We'd opted not to purchase a fancy urn, because they all looked too 'urny', but we weren't expecting him to be in what can only be described as a paper sandwich bag. At least, we thought, if we accidentally drop him we can just vacuum him into a hoover bag and no one would know the difference.

Today, we refer to it as our dad bag, which sends us all into peals of laughter. I often pat the dad bag as I speak to him, wondering if I'm patting his toes, elbows or genitals.

It sounds ludicrous to say that we laughed a lot after his death, but I truly don't think we'd have coped otherwise. My dad was a hilarious man and he wouldn't have wanted it any other way.

Envy

I look at some pictures of an old friend's wedding. It's so lovely. They had the most gorgeous day.

BRAIN: Your dad will never walk you down the aisle.

My friend at work brings in her new baby. He's so cute and tiny.

BRAIN: Your dad will never meet your children.

Sitting in the pub on a Sunday afternoon, a family next to us plays a game of cards.

BRAIN: You will never be a family of four again.

I think envy is the hardest stage of grief. It's like the worst FOMO you could ever experience. Suddenly everything I see is Daddy/Daughter-related in a way I never noticed before. Father's Day comes just a month after his death and feels like a personal attack. I avoid going into supermarkets for an entire two weeks, for fear I will break down in public at the very sight of a Father's Day themed aisle.

Yes, OK, this has happened

Almost a year after my dad died, something came over me. It was like a gust of wind smacking me in the face. I felt the blood run from my head to my toes. He was gone and I'd never, ever get to see him again.

A tsunami of emotions came flooding out of me and I could not stop them. I didn't even try. I let myself wallow in every emotion I was feeling. It didn't feel like a release. It felt suffocating, like nothing could ever console me. Nothing would ever make it better. This empty hole in my heart was never going to be filled, and I would just have to live with it forever.

I've never understood why it took me a whole year to really start to process what had happened. I still find every day hard. I can't speak about him without tearing up. I can't recall memories of us without feeling devastation. I talk to him almost daily and I'm sure my neighbours think I've completely lost the plot, but it somehow makes me feel closer to him. Every bit of big news I thank him for and tell him about, as if he's just on the other end of the phone. It gives me hope that he is nearby and with me at every step. Sometimes when I go to a restaurant one of his favourite songs will play and I'll tell myself it's a message from him. A message that he's with me.

BRAIN: Maybe he is?

My delayed reaction to my dad's death is normal. I knew it would happen, I just didn't know when. Grieving isn't a linear process. You might not follow the SARAH or the HAYLEY method; it's not something we all do at the same pace. It's a unique experience and there's no right or wrong way for it to happen. It may be weeks, months or even years until you're finally able to accept their death, and even then I don't think you'll ever be able to fully accept what has happened.

You probably won't recognise grief in the beginning, but eventually it will all make sense. In the early stages everybody asks if you're OK. You get a month of solid attention, people constantly checking in on you. When that fades you kind of feel like you're a bit of a burden when you talk about it, but you aren't. Death is life-changing. You aren't supposed to just get over it quickly. I'm not sure you ever stop grieving someone you love; I think you just get better at living alongside it. Talking about it helps more than you realise, even just talking about your memories of them. I still love to share stories about my dad, he was one of the biggest lights in my life, and I feel so devastated that not everyone got to meet my hero.

When my dad died, my best friend Immy told me something she'd heard once when a friend of hers passed away. She said, 'When you're in your mother's womb, all you know is her womb, but you're just inches away from a whole other world, one where everyone on the outside knows you exist. Who knows if our loved ones that have passed are just inches away, able to see us still?'

So next time you're having a wank, just remember: all your dead relatives are probably watching you. Sicko.

Brain vs Date

After you've simultaneously gone through a big life change, a break-up with a boyfriend you met abroad and then the loss of a parent, most experts would probably recommend that you don't immediately make any other big life decisions, like getting into a new relationship or switching to decaf coffee. Thankfully I had already made the move away from caffeine a couple of years earlier, but I did decide to stay clear of dating for a while. I wanted to be single and enjoy my own company, which I did, a lot. I very rarely went out. In fact, I spent most of my time in the months after my dad's death snuggled up alone on the sofa at my family home on the Isle of Wight, watching some of the worst TV imaginable. It was exactly what I needed.

As I began to creep back out into the world, I found myself at my friend Sarah's birthday party. It was at the pub, which I thought would be a relatively safe re-introduction to society, and I knew a few old friends would be there. I'd also promised myself that if I didn't like it, I could leave straight away, so I was really bringing the party vibes. Almost as soon as I arrived, Sarah started telling me about how she was also recently single and had only felt like she could move on thanks to a hook-up she'd had shortly after. Her plan was to invite a guy she knew to the pub to meet me that night. I wasn't sure, but I was three margaritas deep, so summoned my famous enthusiasm to say, 'Fine.'

Intensely aware that I was wearing my worst pair of 'grieving pants' – my oldest, holey-est knickers – I suddenly found myself sitting next to a bloke who I can only describe as a *Love Island* contestant. He was around 6ft 5 inches, with the shade of tan you only get out of a bottle, extremely large muscles that protruded through his too-small t-shirt, and eyebrows that were not just overplucked but also dyed a very harsh dark brown. He wasn't my type on paper, but a lot of girls at the pub seemed to be swooning over him.

I didn't know how Sarah had got him down to the pub so quickly, but I think she might have oversold my enthusiasm for a wild night. He was certainly friendly enough. Sadly, I was one of the worst conversationalists of all time. He asked me what my hobbies were (none), what I did for fun (nothing), and what my plans were for the weekend (no plans). He mentioned his dad, at which point I immediately started to cry – big, shuddery, wet tears. He put quite a gentle arm around me and walked me to a taxi, before waving me off. Nice, really. I hope that guy gets what he deserves: a lovely girlfriend, a two-season co-hosting contract on *Love Island: Aftersun*, and a sponsorship deal with a regional personal training gym.

A few months later, while enjoying my favourite hobby of doing nothing on the sofa, a notification pops up on my phone. It's from Hinge. I had a new match! I had been sporadically scrolling through dating apps when I was feeling bored, but not in any serious way. I'd swipe 'yes' on a load of profiles, but I never spoke to anyone or looked at any matches I had. I don't know why this time was different, but I decided to open the match and see who this person was. His name was Damien, he was 31, 6ft 2 inches, worked in advertising, non-smoker, not into drugs, drinks occasionally. He was giving fun-sponge vibes and, you know what, I was feeling it.

Over the next few days, Damien and I messaged loads. At first, I'd wait the customary ten minutes to reply, but honestly, I was really enjoying it. Pretty soon we were talking back and forth like a regular conversation – how retro! We were practically married. He was great, funny, kind and didn't seem like a serial killer. What a catch.

The next day, he asked me if I'd like to grab a drink.

BRAIN: Uh, you're forgetting one small issue.

Oh yeah, I forgot to say, I was catfishing him. It's not like I'd pretended to be someone else. I wasn't posing as a 19-year-old model, or a Nigerian prince with a massive bank account. I had just set my location to London while I was still very much living in the Isle of Wight. In my defence, I'd never planned to meet up with anyone, and I couldn't set my location to the island or all my matches would be the same ten people I went to school with and maybe the *Love Island* guy.

I had to make an excuse as to why I couldn't have a drink, so I told him a little Wight lie (a small lie you tell when you secretly live on the Isle of Wight). I messaged: *Ah, so sorry! Would have loved to grab a drink. I'm actually on the Isle of Wight over the next few weeks for work. Maybe when I'm back in London?*

> BRAIN: Genius! Right, so what are we going to do when he asks again in a few weeks?

I hadn't thought this through. I wasn't ready to move back to London just yet, and certainly not for one date with a guy from Hinge . . . or was I? I opened Rightmove and looked for flats to rent. As expected, there was nothing bigger than a shoebox in my budget, plus I remembered I probably shouldn't move to a city just for a date.

Two weeks passed and we spoke a fair amount. Not so much that we'd ruin the mystery, but enough for me to gather a few minor facts about him, enabling me to conduct an extremely thorough online investigation of his entire life. Honestly, I should work for the government. I knew where he worked, where he lived, what his family looked like, how long he'd been in London and, of course, who his ex-girlfriend was. From his end, the only thing he really knew about me was that I definitely lived in London.

BRAIN: Just tell him! If he likes us enough it won't matter.

I figured I had nothing to lose. I message him: I can't believe I'm admitting this, but I've catfished you. My name is Hayley, I am exactly who I say I am, nothing else is false, but I don't live in London.

There's a pause. He leaves me on read for about three minutes; it feels like an age. Then the typing bubble appears. As I wait, my breath quickens, my heart races and I wonder if he is about to tell me to fuck off.

BRAIN: He's definitely typing something rude, he's for sure angry with us.

The reply popped up onto my screen: I knew it!!! Who works in comedy and needs to go to the Isle of Wight for a completely random amount of time? Did you ever have any intention of going for a drink?

He seemed OK – not mad, just a bit confused. I explained why I had set my location to London and how I was eventually planning to move back. In fact, I'd already decided I was going to head there to see some friends in about a month's time. He asked if I wanted to get a drink then.

*

The month passes and I'm at my friend Lucy's house trying to decide what to wear. I've brought a massive suitcase for my short trip for this exact reason. It's filled with outfits that show off my nipples (not on purpose) and also my toes, just in case he's a feet guy. I haven't decided if I'm OK with him being a feet guy, but I want to cover all bases.

BRAIN: Why are you so anxious? It's just a date.

Totally. It is just a date. I've been on dates before.

BRAIN: But it could also be the most important date of our entire life.

No date should feel this stressful. I think it's because we've been chatting for so long, the pressure has really mounted. I try on jeans and a shirt, but it looks way too casual, and then a dress, which is way too formal. I'm sending pictures to every WhatsApp group I know to gather my friends' opinions – 30 unqualified personal stylists working overtime to tell me I'm both over- and underdressed to go to the pub with a guy I don't even really know.

BRAIN: I think we should cancel.

HEART: We can't cancel! What if he's the one? Next year we'll be married and living in a huge house with loads of plants and dancing around our tidy kitchen together.

UTERUS: With our ten kids! For goodness sake, don't forget the kids!

Heart and Uterus always picture me in a Nancy Meyers movie. Vagina pictures me in the gutter.

VAGINA: Let's just fuck him and chuck him. We're on the road to bang-town, baby, this one's a sure thing!

Enough. I feel like I'm going to throw up or shit myself, maybe both. I don't think I've ever been this nervous in my life. What if all this time I thought I catfished him, but he really catfished me? Time is running out, so I block out the noise and pick an outfit that accidentally becomes my biggest fashion faux pas. Not only are my toes out, but my top is so see-through and not the type you can wear a bra with, so you can also see my nipples. I did try nipple covers but it kind of looked like I was smuggling honey-roast ham slices down my top, so now I'm hopping into the taxi with my double Ts – tits and toes – out for the world to see.

Three minutes later, I consider getting out of the taxi. I can't do this. I feel so awkward and silly. Maybe I'm just not ready to meet anyone.

BRAIN: What do we actually have to lose?

I mean, nothing.

BRAIN: Didn't all the good things we've done
start out feeling scary?

Yeah, but what if this doesn't work out? What if he
doesn't like me? What if I don't like him? This could all
go tits over toes!

BRAIN: So what? We're fine on our own, we
already know that much.

We are fine on our own. I hate how right she is. I don't
have anything to lose. But I can't shake the nerves. I
message Damien: I'm on my way but I'm really, really
nervous :)

He replies: Me too! Don't worry. I'm sitting outside, I'll
see you when you get here.

Right at that moment, the driver pulls up at the back of
the pub. I spot Damien – he's exactly who he says he is.
In fact, he's really good-looking, much better than his
pictures. He looks up and we make direct eye contact. I
raise a hand to wave. He smiles. Then the taxi pulls away,
with me still inside it.

The driver mutters, 'I'm just going to drop you round
the front.'

BRAIN: Oh my God, he's going to think you
took one look at him and left!

I'm panicking. I don't know what to do. At the front of the pub, I pay the driver, rush out of the taxi, call Lucy and ask what to do. She tells me to run around the back. I shuffle round in my stupid, glorified flip-flops as my nipples try to make their escape. This pub is unreasonably huge. Who would even build a pub this big? Does it ever get full? When I finally reach the table, humiliatingly out of breath – and doing everything I can not to show it – Damien is standing with his jacket in his arms. I screech, 'Are you leaving?'

He laughs, 'I was coming to find you.'

The rest of the evening is nice. Really nice. I drink a few too many gin and tonics and relax a bit (eventually). At the end of the night, we say our goodbyes and never see each other again. Just kidding! We've been together ever since and hopefully we're still together when you're reading this.

Oh and, no, turns out he's not a toe guy.

Me vs Therapy

Before I went to therapy I had a lot of misconceptions about what it would be like. I figured it would involve me laying on a chaise longue, detailing my weird sex dreams. I thought the therapist would be an incredibly old man, who stroked his beard as he silently judged everything I said. Mostly, I thought therapy existed to catch you out. I'd imagined that if you said one wrong word, you'd be shipped straight off to a Victorian asylum. I didn't ever think of it as something that could actually be helpful.

As I reached the latter part of my 20s, I started to wonder if it might be useful to talk to someone other than Brain about everything that was bothering me. Maybe even to check whether Brain knew what she was talking about. When I'd first started having panic attacks almost a decade ago, my doctor had suggested I try it. I wasn't ready then – I just didn't see what it could do for me. I had tried it on one occasion before, but it had seemed too overwhelming, so I just gave up. But recently I'd begun to realise that all my friends were doing it. Maybe it was cool to sort out all of your childhood trauma? Plus I'm pretty sure that having to grieve your dad before he died and then again after he died was something I should probably talk to a professional about.

The first step into therapy is finding a therapist. This part is hard; the choice is huge. It's like doing an assault course backwards, assuming that the hardest part of the course is at the end. Honestly, I don't know how assault courses work. I'm more into Easter Egg hunts and things that end in reward, not pain. I started my search with a list – they had to live close to me, be over a certain age, and I didn't want us to have any mutual friends. These aren't hard and fast rules, they're just what I had in mind when I started browsing. Finding a therapist is like dating, in that you're definitely going to be disappointed most of the time, but if you find the right one, they *can* fix you (please know I am joking. No one can fix you; you're not broken!).

Quickly, my parameters changed. I found myself judging therapists by the way they posed for a picture. Did I want a happy therapist or a serious therapist? A man or a woman? A white shirt or a floofy blouse? I decided I wanted a woman, over 40 and, frankly, I wanted her to be a bit mumsy-looking.

BRAIN: Why don't you just talk to our mum? It would be cheaper. Plus, she already knows about our childhood trauma, she was there.

No, I wanted to talk to someone who didn't know anything about me. Who wouldn't judge me, or have any preconceptions about who I am. My mum gives great advice, but I didn't want advice. I just wanted to talk.

After a lot of searching, and a lot of rejection emails (thank goodness I didn't have a problem with rejection or I'd need two therapists, one to get over the emails and another for all the other stuff) I think I've found the one. She has a nice smile, a good blouse, and she specialises in both bereavement and anxiety – the Venn diagram of champions. I book an appointment, and two days later head to a tall building tucked behind the high street to meet Marie.

Before I go in, I have to fill out a self-evaluation questionnaire. Immediately, I lie. I lie about my job. I lie about how happy I am. I lie about my home address. I almost lie about my name, but I realise my email stated both my first and last name, and if I did that she might think I was suffering the same affliction as my dad.

BRAIN: No, you're doing it right. Tell her nothing. Then she'll have no way of blackmailing us with all our deepest darkest secrets!

A few minutes later, she waves me in and asks me to take a seat opposite her. She's exactly how she looks in her pictures, down to the smile. I immediately feel comfortable in her presence. She flicks through my questionnaire, before looking at me, puzzled, 'It's unusual to conduct couples therapy for a single person.'

I agree. 'Well, you see the thing is, Brain and I, we aren't getting on very well.'

I can see I've alarmed her by referring to Brain and I as a 'we', but she humours me. She asks me what exactly brought me here.

I want to tell her that I am crippled with grief. I feel like I haven't processed my father's death, nor the fact that he had dementia. That I feel numb inside and for the past few years of my life have been doing everything I can to distract myself as Brain tells me to kiss my uni lecturer, kick babies and drive off cliffs.

Instead, I tell her, 'Oh, you know, just the normal stuff.' She wants me to be more specific.

BRAIN: No way. You've told her quite enough. Do you know how bad that makes me look? Don't embarrass me like that!

In that moment, I decide that maybe after years of feeling embarrassed and surviving it, Brain can handle a little more. I start talking, and I can't stop. I tell Marie everything – about my dad, my past break-ups, my crippling self-doubt, everything about Brain, the lot. I don't leave out a single detail. It comes tumbling out of my mouth like word vomit.

She pauses, 'And do you think what you've been feeling is normal?'

Do I think what I've been feeling is normal? I don't know. It's certainly what I've lived with every single day, but do other people feel this way? I can't be the only person in the world to have such bad anxiety that even standing first in line at a busy post office feels embarrassing.

I answer, 'Yes.'

BRAIN: Great. Now you've done it, she's going to call for a white van to come and get us. We're off to Bedlam, baby!

Marie reassures me that it is indeed perfectly normal. She tells me anxiety and grief and stress can make you behave and feel all kinds of things. She asks me about my childhood and when I first remember Brain becoming so loud.

BRAIN: Wow, she's really buying into the whole, 'I'm the villain' bit, isn't she?

As the session goes by, I find I've overshared every last detail with this woman. I've got snot oozing out of my nose, and I've made my way through her entire pack of tissues. As I speak, she says things like, 'That must have been really hard,' and, 'I'm sorry you felt that way.'

It's validating how she looks at me, how she talks to me, and I feel as if I was ever to tell her something awful, she'd continue her sympathetic looks, but while we're speaking, nothing feels that awful.

Just before we wrap up, she draws a little diagram on

a whiteboard and unpacks the chaos of my life. She tries to figure out where one thing leads into another and what the root of all my problems is. She sends me away with some worksheets for Brain and I to complete before our next session. Every night that week, instead of arguing with Brain, we sit together and fill them out.

> BRAIN: You know, it's really nice to be asked something about myself for once.

I agree.

Me and Brain

If you're reading this, it's because I'm dead.

Just kidding! I'm alive. At least, I think I'm alive. If you're reading this and I am actually dead, then please tell my mum I love her and also definitely don't look in the drawer of my bedside table. Just throw the whole thing out – it's better that way, seriously.

Welcome to the conclusion of my book. We did it! I wrote a whole book and you read one – well done us! What a nice time we've had together. Remember when I nearly died from a ballistic missile attack? Or when I nearly drove my car off that cliff?

> BRAIN: Or when you nearly died and had to go to A&E and it turned out you weren't dying at all? That was a fun waste of literally everyone's time.

Yup, fun stuff all round! There were poop-related incidents, break-ups and breakthroughs, but nothing prepared either of us for losing a parent. We've been through a lot together, haven't we, Brain?

BRAIN: We sure have. In fact, seeing it all written out, I think I need another holiday.

Maybe we can pop you in that jar on my desk and pickle you now?

Losing my dad at 28 years old was one of the hardest, most pivotal moments of my life. And somehow this book turned into a form of therapy for me. I was forced to go back over times that I perhaps didn't want to think about. Sure, there were lots of tears, but you should see the cute crying-selfies I got out of it.

At times, writing this book made me feel very self-conscious, but whenever it did, I'd think about a piece of advice my wonderful dad once gave me: Do whatever you want to do. Who cares if people think you're weird? If it's fun for you, just do it. You'll probably never see any of them ever again, so who even cares?

BRAIN: Hey, that *is* good advice.

I never used to think of Brain as someone I liked, she was just a nuisance. She's spent most of my life encouraging me to feel guilty, embarrassed and scared. But today, as I sit in a crowded café around the corner from my home, I notice that I've recently started to feel a little bit better. Brain still has her routines, but I'm less worried about them now. After spending my life trying to silence her, I realise that not only is it not possible, but it's also not necessary. In fact, sometimes it's even good to listen to her.

BRAIN: I told you! I'm always right!

You're not always right, but that's OK, too. No one's right all the time.

These days, I try to talk about Brain with other people. A lot. It turns out, it's not just me who has this incredibly overactive Brain. Loads of us do. We think the whole world is watching us while we wait to cross at the traffic lights, we share a sudden urge to bite our dentist's rubbery gloved finger, and we've even pictured hurling ourselves in front of a moving train (one of the intrusive thoughts I am most scared to talk about; it feels the most taboo). But these are normal, human feelings, not something to be ashamed of, and most of the time it's Brain's way of protecting us from bad situations. She just chooses to do it in a really avant-garde way.

At the same time, I've come to understand that sometimes these thoughts and feelings are just Brain stuff. They're not me – who I really am or what I really feel. If you're having thoughts and feelings that concern you, you should reach out and talk to someone about getting help. Brain might try to make you feel like this isn't possible, but that's Brain's problem, not yours. Therapy ended up being one of the best things I ever did for myself. I put it off for a long time for a number of reasons, but my only regret now is not starting it earlier. We've all got to learn to care for our grey, blubbery brains like the mad little animals they are.

I'll never be completely free from Brain. We're in it together for life. Sure, she's quieter than she used to be, but she can still make me feel panicky, shy or worried at a moment's notice. Sometimes, though, she'll throw me a compliment, an idea or a really good memory, and I think Brain and I . . . yeah, we're friends.

BRAIN: We sure are, I've always got your back.

Acknowledgements

I don't have a clue how to do this part. I'm incredibly awkward when it comes to being sentimental and heartfelt – I usually adopt an Australian accent for times like these, so please do read this in your best Aussie accent, as it was intended.

Firstly, I'd like to thank my incredible dad, Kevin Morris, for everything he taught me in life, for introducing me to the world of comedy and always being there for me through the good and bad – you really were the best dad a girl could have asked for. I'd like to thank my mum for all the great advice, and for being such a cheerleader through all those moments in my life when I had no fucking idea what I was doing. And my brother, who is the funniest person I know (funnier than me by a long shot) for all the silliness in our childhood and for being such a rock when we lost our wonderful dad.

To Zennor, my editor, for helping me birth this book, through all my tears and, 'I don't think I can do this, it's shit' messages. And to Charlie, who helped me wade through the shitstorm of editing my word vomit.

To 'Damien', for being such a constant through the writing of this book, and for all the delicious dinners that fuelled it. To my best friend Immy, who endured lengthy voice notes and long chats. To Ella, for being such a support in my life.

I'd like to thank my agents Milly and Stan along with everyone at InterTalent (if that doesn't make me sound like too much of a wannabe diva), for everything.

Finally, I want to thank you. My life has changed dramatically since 2021 and I am the happiest I have been in such a long time. It's an absolute privilege to be able to wake up and do a job that fills me with so much joy every single day. The community we have built online feels like my comfort place, where we can all feel normal and rejoice in having similar, annoying brains. None of this would be possible without you. Thank you, thank you, thank you.